Learn Every Day About Numbers

Edited by Kathy Charner

Learn Every Day About NUMBERS

BEST IDEAS from TEACHERS

EDITED BY
Kathy Charner

© 2009 Gryphon House, Inc.
Published by Gryphon House, Inc.
P.O. Box 207, Beltsville, MD 20704
800.638.0928; 301.595.9500; 301.595.0051 (fax)

Visit us on the web at www.gryphonhouse.com

Illustrations: Deb Johnson
Cover Art: Stock photos

Library of Congress Cataloging-in-Publication Information:
Learn every day about numbers / edited by Kathy Charner.
     p. cm.
 ISBN 978-0-87659-090-4
1. Arithmetic--Study and teaching (Preschool)--Activity programs. 2.
Education, Preschool--Activity programs. I. Charner, Kathy.
 QA135.6.L33 2009
 518'.45--dc22

                              2008054620

BULK PURCHASE

Gryphon House books are available for special premiums and sales promotions as well as for fund-raising use. Special editions or book excerpts also can be created to specification. For details, contact the Director of Marketing at Gryphon House.

DISCLAIMER

Gryphon House, Inc. and the authors cannot be held responsible for damage, mishap, or injury incurred during the use of or because of activities in this book. Appropriate and reasonable caution and adult supervision of children involved in activities and corresponding to the age and capability of each child involved is recommended at all times. Do not leave children unattended at any time. Observe safety and caution at all times.

Table of Contents

Note: The books listed in the Related Children's Books section of each activity may occasionally include books that are only available used or through your local library.

Introduction

You have in your hands a great teacher resource! This book, which is part of the *Learn Every Day* series, contains 100 activities you can use with children ages 3–6 to help them develop a lifelong love of learning, as well as the knowledge and skills all children need to become successful students in kindergarten and beyond. The activities in this book are written by teachers and professionals from the field of early childhood education—educators and professionals who use these activities in their classrooms every day.

The activities in this book are separated by curriculum areas, such as Circle or Group Time, Dramatic Play, Outdoor Play, Small Motor, and so on, and are organized according to their age appropriateness, so activities appropriate for children ages three and up come first, then activities appropriate for children age four and up, and finally, activities for children age five and up. Each activity has the following components—learning objectives, a list of related vocabulary words, a list of thematically related books, a list of the materials (if any) you need to complete the activity, directions for preparation, and the activity itself. Also included in each activity is an assessment component to help you observe how well the children are meeting the learning objectives. Given the emphasis on accountability in early childhood education, these assessment strategies are essential.

Several activities also contain teacher-to-teacher tips that provide smart and useful ideas, including how to expand the central idea of an activity in a new way or where to find the materials necessary to complete a given activity. Some activities also include related fingerplays, poems, or songs that you can sing and chant with the children. Children love singing, dancing, and chanting—actions that help expand children's understanding of an activity's learning objectives.

This book, and the other books in this series, give early childhood educators 100 great activities that require few materials, little if any preparation, and are sure to make learning fun and engaging for children.

Block Mania

5+

LEARNING OBJECTIVES

The children will:
1. Create block structures.
2. Count objects from 1–10.
3. Write numbers from 1–10 following an example.

Materials

blocks: wooden,
    cardboard,
    foam, colored,
    alphabet, unit
accessories: traffic
    signs, stores,
    people and
    animal figures
paper
pencils
number cards

VOCABULARY

| blocks | long | stack |
| build | short | tall |

PREPARATION

● Create a project sharing form that the children will fill out. The form should say, "I built a(n) _____ and used _____ (number) blocks." Leave room for the children to draw their object. Copy enough forms for each child.

WHAT TO DO

1. Designate a space for the block structures that the children will create. In the block area, provide a variety of blocks. Include traffic signs, stores, people, and animal figures in your block area.
2. Tell the children that it is time for Block Mania. Give the children plenty of time to explore the materials.
3. When the children, in groups or individually, have created a structure they want to keep for a while and share with others, they can use the project sharing form. Help the children fill out the form.
4. Have the children give a name to their block structure. Help the children write their names on the form.
5. Have the children count the blocks they used and write that number on the form using the models provided. Place the block structure in a special area.
6. Keep the children's creations on display that week, so they can look and share with one another.

ASSESSMENT

To assess the children's learning, consider the following:
● When given a number of objects, can the children count out 10 of them?
● When given written examples of the numbers 1–10, can the children copy the numbers?

Children's Books

Learning Block Books: Numbers, Colors, Shapes, Animals by Susan Estelle Kwas
Spot's Colors, Shapes, and Numbers by Eric Hill
Ten Black Dots by Donald Crews

Monica Hay Cook, Tucson, AZ

Number Detective

3+

LEARNING OBJECTIVES

The children will:
1. Enjoy books.
2. Search for and identify numbers.
3. Role-play.
4. Develop their language skills.

Materials

fabric paint,
    markers, or
    number stickers
baseball cap
assortment of
    number and
    counting books
magnifying glass

VOCABULARY

find	magnifying glass	read
hat	numbers	search

PREPARATION

● Use the paint, markers, or stickers to add random number on the baseball cap to create a Number Detective hat.

WHAT TO DO

1. Invite a child to put on the cap and pick up the magnifying glass.
2. Give the child an assortment of number and counting books.
3. Encourage the child to use the magnifying glass to search through the books to find numbers.
4. When the child locates numbers on the pages of the books, she should let you know.

TEACHER-TO-TEACHER TIP

● An easy alternative for the detective hat is to write numbers on squares of colorful paper and tape or glue them to a baseball cap.

ASSESSMENT

To assess the children's learning, consider the following:
● Give the children an assortment of number and counting books. Can each child identify numbers 1–10 on the pages in the book?
● Hide numbers around the room. Can the children find the numbers in the room?
● Display several sheets of newspaper ads. Can the children identify numbers and circle them on the pages?

Children's Books

Annie's One to Ten by
    Annie Owen
Counting Sheep by
    John Archambault
*There Were Ten in the
    Bed* by Annie Kubler

Mary J. Murray, Mazomanie, WI

Corduroy's Pocket

4+

LEARNING OBJECTIVES

The children will:
1. Learn to recognize numbers.
2. Learn to count actions to match a number.

Materials

Corduroy's Pocket
   by Don Freeman
number cards for
   1–5
tagboard
glue
markers
piece of corduroy
   fabric

VOCABULARY

corduroy   number names   pocket

PREPARATION

● Make number cards from 4″ x 6″ tagboard. Write the numbers 1–5.
● Make a tagboard pocket at least 6″ x 8″. Glue three edges together and write "Corduroy's Pocket" on the front. Slip the number cards inside.

WHAT TO DO

1. Read *Corduroy's Pocket* by Don Freeman to the children several times. Put a copy in the book area for the children to read independently.
2. Show the pocket to the children. Invite a child to come and draw a number card out of "Corduroy's pocket." Ask the child to name the number on the card.
3. Ask all the children to clap that number of times.
4. Vary the actions with slapping their knees, snapping their fingers, patting their shoes, and so on.
5. When the children are ready, use cards from 1–10.

ASSESSMENT

To assess the children's learning, consider the following:
● Show the children the set of number cards individually. Can the children name the cards when they are in random order?
● Can the children choose a card, name the number, and clap the correct number of times?

Susan Oldham Hill, Lakeland, FL

Children's Books

Corduroy by
   Don Freeman
My Little Counting Book
   by Roger Priddy
A Pocket for Corduroy
   by Don Freeman

The Numeral Song

4+

LEARNING OBJECTIVES

The children will:

1. Learn how to form numerals.
2. Develop number recognition.

Materials

recording of "The
   Numeral Song"
   from *Sing to
   Learn with Dr.
   Jean*
tape or CD player
oak tag
copy paper
marker or
   computer

VOCABULARY

number names, to 10   numeral

PREPARATION

- Make a book with the lyrics from Dr. Jean's "The Numeral Song."
- Write the numbers, one on each page, with arrows to illustrate the correct formation of each number from 1–10.

WHAT TO DO

1. Play a recording of "The Numeral Song."
2. Hold the book up so that all the children can see the number.
3. Demonstrate how to make the number by tracing the number on the page.
4. Encourage the children to draw the figures in the air with large strokes to help them practice writing numbers and remember the correct formation as you sing the song together.

TEACHER-TO-TEACHER TIP

- If "The Numeral Song" is not available, the Internet has several sites with rhymes to help the children write their numbers.

ASSESSMENT

To assess the children's learning, consider the following:

- Can children correctly form numbers?
- Can children write numbers 1–10?

Jackie Wright, Enid, OK

Children's Books

Count and See by
   Tana Hoban
*Fish E: A Book You Can
   Count On* by
   Lois Ehlert
Ten Black Dots by
   Donald Crews

Songs

"Ten in the Bed"
"This Old Man"

Straight and Curvy Numbers Book

Materials

- craft sticks
- yarn
- card stock (6" x 6"; several per child)
- glue sticks
- stapler
- plastic bags (10 per child)
- number stickers (optional)

LEARNING OBJECTIVES

The children will:
1. Learn the difference between numbers that are made from straight or curved lines and numbers that include both (a good activity for tactile learners).
2. Learn to form numbers.

VOCABULARY

curved   number names   straight

PREPARATION

- Cut craft sticks into short pieces for numbers with straight lines, such as 1, 4, and 7.
- Cut yarn pieces for numbers with curved lines such as 2, 3, 5, 6, 8, and 9. The length will depend on how big you want the children to make the numbers. For 6" x 6" card stock, make the yarn pieces 4" long.
- Put the craft sticks and yarn into individual bags. Prepare enough that there is one bag per number per child.

WHAT TO DO

1. Let the children explore the craft sticks or yarn, forming them into numbers (one per piece of card stock).
2. Ask the children to take the glue stick and "write" the number on the card stock. Smaller children will need help with this.
3. Place the craft sticks or yarn over the glue, forming the number. Allow to dry.
4. When the pages are completely dried, staple two more pieces of plain card stock to the front and back, forming a book.
5. The children can decorate the cover with stickers of numbers or draw them. Write "My Number Book" on the cover if desired.

TEACHER-TO-TEACHER TIP

- Bulky yarn works best for this activity.

ASSESSMENT

To assess the children's learning, consider the following:
- Can the children recognize number "shapes"?
- Do the children understand the concepts of straight and curved?

Children's Books

Neil's Numberless World by Lucy Coats
Numberlies: Number One by Colin and Jacqui Hawkins (a series of book featuring numbers 1–10)
Spot's Colors, Shapes, and Numbers by Eric Hill

Donna Alice Patton, Hillsboro, OH

Ten Little Rabbits

4+

LEARNING OBJECTIVES

The children will:
1. Count units in a group.
2. Describe some traditional Native-American activities.
3. Tap a steady beat to a chant.

Materials

Ten Little Rabbits
by Virginia
Grossman

VOCABULARY

anglers   plain   trappers   weavers
beat

PREPARATION

- Practice reading the book as a rhythmic chant while tapping the beat.

WHAT TO DO

1. With the children, look at each picture in the book. Count the number of rabbits in that picture and discuss the rabbits' activity (the pages in the back of the book describe each activity).
2. Read the book to the children. Invite the children to start each page with you by saying the number of rabbits on that page.
3. Repeat step two until children come in with the number on cue as you maintain a rhythmic chant while reading.
4. Start tapping a steady beat on your thighs and invite the children to do the same. While they are tapping, read the book in a rhythmic chant.
   Note: You may prefer to have the children lightly tap their toes or pat their fingers together.
5. Finally, ask the children to say the number at the beginning of each page while you rhythmically read the book and they tap or pat the beat.
   Note: Your class can "perform" the book for families, or for another class or teacher.

ASSESSMENT

To assess the children's learning, consider the following:
- Randomly open to a page in the book. Can the children tell you how many rabbits are in the picture?
- Act out one of the activities pictured in the book (fishing, weaving, tracking). Can the children identify the activity?

Roberta Volkmann, Springfield, IL

Children's Books

Chicka Chicka Boom Boom by Bill Martin, Jr.
Over in the Meadow by John Langstaff
Ten Little Rabbits by Virginia Grossman

Baggie Book

5+

LEARNING OBJECTIVES

The children will:
1. Save favorite numbers in an organized "baggie book."
2. Draw pictures representing favorite numbers.
3. Read or recite favorite numbers out loud.
4. Use favorite numbers as a "dictionary" or reference for spelling and writing favorite numbers.

Materials

plastic sandwich
  baggies (at least
  two per child)
paper
any drawing tools:
  crayons, markers,
  colored pencils
any writing tool:
  pen, pencil, or
  marker
stapler or single
  metal ring
hole punch,
  optional

VOCABULARY

dictation	drawing	literacy	writing
dictionary	favorite	reading	

PREPARATION

● Cut squares of drawing paper to fit inside a clear plastic sandwich baggie, and keep in a box in the child's art or writing area.
● Keep paper squares, baggies, and drawing tools on hand for children to draw or write favorite numbers whenever they choose.

WHAT TO DO

1. Ask the children to draw a set of items that represents their favorite number.
2. Help the children write the number word next to their picture. Put each child's favorite number drawing into a clear sandwich baggie and close it.
3. When there are two or more favorite word baggies, staple them together like a book. Or, if preferred, punch a single hole in the strong part of the baggie and insert a single metal binder ring. The ring method allows for words to be added or removed easily.
4. Each baggie can have a word facing front, and one facing back, that is, two drawings/words per baggie.
5. Place the baggies in an easily accessible place in the classroom.

ASSESSMENT

To assess the children's learning, consider the following:
● Can the children memorize the spelling of their favorite number word is as it relates to the drawing?
● Can each child refer to her favorite word baggies when she needs help spelling a word?

MaryAnn Kohl, Bellingham, WA

Children's Books

My Favorite Word Book
  by Selina Young
Spot's Favorite Words
  by Eric Hill
*The Very Hungry
Caterpillar's Favorite
Words* by Eric Carle

Class Lift-the-Flap Book

5+

LEARNING OBJECTIVES

The children will:

1. Learn to name the numbers 1–5.
2. Learn to make sets for numbers 1–5.

Materials

9" x 12"
  construction
  paper in assorted
  colors
markers
hole punch
4" x 7" card stock
glue
number cards for
  1–5
metal rings (or
  yarn) for
  assembling the
  book
small blocks or
  counters

VOCABULARY

count   flap   set

PREPARATION

● Draw a line down the middle of each sheet of 9" x 12" construction paper, positioned horizontally.
● Punch holes in the left side of the paper.
● Fold the 4" x 7" card stock along the short edge, making a ¼" fold for gluing.

WHAT TO DO

1. Show the children the number cards for 1–5. Explain that they will be coloring sets of objects that match these numbers to make a lift-the-flap book for the classroom.
2. Give each child a sheet of 9" x 12" construction paper, positioned horizontally with the holes punched on the left. Ask the children to choose a number card, name the number, and draw a set of that many objects on the right side of their papers. Ask the children to try to keep the objects on the right side of the line.
3. When the children are finished drawing, ask them to count the objects. Write the number (no larger than 4" x 7") on the left side of the page and glue a card stock covering for the number to make a flap to lift. Allow to dry.
4. Assemble the pages in numerical order with a cover sheet and slip the rings through the holes.

ASSESSMENT

To assess the children's learning, consider the following:
● Can the children recognize the numbers on the cards?
● Using small blocks or counters, can the children make sets to match the number cards?

Susan Oldham Hill, Lakeland, FL

Children's Books

Anno's Counting House
  by Mitsumasa Anno
Count! by Denise
  Fleming
How Many Snails? by
  Paul Giganti, Jr.

Number Book

5+

LEARNING OBJECTIVES

The children will:
1. Count numbers.
2. Create a book of numbers.
3. Decorate their book.

Materials

poster of numbers
  from 1–10
copy paper
paper numbers
crayons
markers

VOCABULARY

number names to 10

PREPARATION

- Place a poster of numbers from 1–10 on the wall in the classroom.
- Put five sheets of copy paper together. Fold in half. Staple the fold to create a "number book."
- Make one book for each child.

WHAT TO DO

1. Point to each number on the poster. Ask the children to identify each number. Count with them.
2. Pass out the number books. Give each child his own set of paper numbers.
3. Ask the children to glue the numbers in the book. Ask them to place each number on a separate page. Give them crayons and markers to draw in their books.
4. Say, "Draw one thing on the 'one' page. Draw two things on the 'two' page, and so on."
5. Help the children write their names on the back page of their books.

TEACHER-TO-TEACHER TIP

- Ask the children to say the numbers as they glue them in their book. Use other props such as posters to visually reinforce the numbers.

ASSESSMENT

To assess the children's learning, consider the following:
- Can the children tell you about their number books?
- Can the children tell you what numbers they see?
- Can the children count together?

Lily Erlic, Victoria, British Columbia, Canada

Children's Books

Numbers 1–10 by Lois Bottoni
One Little Bench: Numbers 1–10 by Joan Hoffman
Ten Black Dots by Donald Crews

Animal Sizing

3+

LEARNING OBJECTIVES

The children will:

1. Make size comparisons.
2. Practice counting.
3. Reinforce their understanding of size comparison terms.
4. Practice estimating.

Materials

supply of toy animals (stuffed, plastic, wooden) for children who do not bring one from home

VOCABULARY

big	biggest	smaller
bigger	small	smallest

PREPARATION

● Beforehand, send a note home to families, asking them to let their children bring in a toy animal.

WHAT TO DO

1. Ask the children to sit in a circle with their animals in front of them.
2. Provide a toy animal from your supply for those who did not bring one to class.
3. Ask the children to look at all the animals, and ask which are biggest and smallest. This is usually a huge stuffed toy and a tiny plastic animal. Put these animals at opposite ends of the workspace.
4. Encourage the children to choose the next biggest animal, until you have a line of animals sorted according to their size.
5. Give the children as much help as is appropriate for their age. If they are having difficulty, ask the children to compare the animal to the last in the line and ask, "Is your animal bigger or smaller than that one?"
6. Count the number of children in unison with the class.
7. Ask the children if there are more, less, or the same number of animals than children.

ASSESSMENT

To assess the children's learning, consider the following:

● Can the children make correct size comparisons?
● Can the children count up to the correct number of children?
● Do the children understand the size comparison terms?
● Can the children estimate that there will be the same number of animals as children?

Children's Books

Big and Little by by Bobbie Kalman
Size by Henry Arthur Pluckrose

Poem

"Little Miss Muffet"

Anne Adeney, Plymouth, England, United Kingdom

1, 2, 3, Line Up

4+

LEARNING OBJECTIVES

The children will:
1. Learn to count to five.
2. Learn to put numbers in order.

Materials

12" x 18" cards for
numbers 1–5

VOCABULARY

number names 1–5   observation   order

WHAT TO DO

1. Choose five children to stand in front of the group, holding the number cards so all the children can see them. Help the children get in the correct order.
2. Ask the remaining children to close their eyes. While their eyes are closed, move one of the five children out of order.
3. Tell the children to open their eyes and discover who is out of order. When someone names the child and the order is restored, count out loud from one to five as a group.
4. Repeat the activity, moving a different child out of order. After several turns, choose a new set of children to hold the cards.

TEACHER-TO-TEACHER TIP

- Tape some numbers to classroom items for the children to put in order: chairs, trucks, crayon containers. Add numbers 6–10 after the children are able to work successfully with 1–5.

Children's Books

Fun with Counting by
Jenny Ackland
How Many Snails? by
Paul Giganti, Jr.
This Old Man by
Tony Ross

ASSESSMENT

To assess the children's learning, consider the following:
- Can each child put the number cards in the correct order?
- Can the children easily find which child is out of order?

Susan Oldham Hill, Lakeland, FL

Christmas Tree Math

4+

LEARNING OBJECTIVES

The children will:

1. Learn to recognize the numbers 1–6 (or higher for older children).
2. Learn to count the correct number of items to match the number.

Materials

3'–4' artificial tree
small bag
5" number cards
labeled 1–6 (or
higher for older
children)
container
25 small
unbreakable
ornaments with
yarn loops

VOCABULARY

number   set

WHAT TO DO

1. Teach the children the following song:

   My Little Christmas Tree by Susan Oldham Hill
   (Tune: "I'm a Little Teapot")
   My little Christmas tree is empty and bare,
   No decorations hanging there.
   Please pull out a card
   And then we'll see
   How many decorations go on my tree.

2. Show the children the tree and choose a child to begin decorating it.
3. Ask the child to draw a number card from the bag and identify it.
4. Choose a second child to count out the matching number of decorations from the container.
5. As a group, count the set of decorations before the children hang them on the tree to make sure the amount is correct.
6. Ask the two children to hang them on the tree.
7. Sing the song again as the next child chooses a number card.

TEACHER-TO-TEACHER TIP

- After the children have used the tree several times in a directed activity, put the tree out for them to use as they choose.

ASSESSMENT

To assess the children's learning, consider the following:

- While the children are drawing cards and counting items, can they identify the numbers on the cards and count rationally?
- Do the children understand the concept of zero?

Susan Oldham Hill, Lakeland, FL

Children's Books

Count and See by Tana Hoban
Moja Means One by Muriel Feelings
Mouse Count by Ellen Stoll Walsh
A Tree Is Nice by Janice May Udry

Count Around the Circle

4+

LEARNING OBJECTIVES

The children will:

1. Reinforce counting and listening skills.
2. Learn to pay attention.

Materials

individual cushions or place mats (optional)

VOCABULARY

number names   one by one

WHAT TO DO

1. Sit in a circle with the children and ask them, "How many people are here today? Let's count!"
2. Look into the eyes of the child to your right and say, "one." She should turn her head, look at the child to her right, and say "two."
3. Continue around the circle and at the end, ask, "How many people are here today?" The children should respond with the correct number.
4. Another variation is to ask each child to say the number plus his name when it is his turn.

TEACHER-TO-TEACHER TIPS

- Ask the children to pass a soft toy around as they say their number.
- Consider adding an element of excitement by using an electronic timer to check the duration of the count. See if the children can count around the circle faster on second and third attempts.

ASSESSMENT

To assess the children's learning, consider the following:

- Can each child understand that she must listen to her neighbor to know what number she has to say?
- Can the children play this game at a faster pace?

Patrick Mitchell, Yagoto, Nagoya, Japan

Children's Books

I Spy Little Numbers by Jean Marzollo
My Little Counting Book by Roger Priddy
Wheels All Around by Anne Lawrence

Flashlight Writer

4+

LEARNING OBJECTIVES
The children will:
1. Learn to write numbers.
2. Learn to recognize numbers.

Materials

chalkboard
chalk
flashlight

VOCABULARY
number names   trace   write

PREPARATION
- Draw large numbers from 1–5 on the chalkboard. Make the number about 3' tall.

WHAT TO DO
1. Turn out the lights. Show the children how to turn on the flashlight and "write" on one of the numbers drawn on the chalkboard. Demonstrate how to move the flashlight slowly over the numbers to trace over the lines on the board.
2. Ask a child to choose a number and hold the flashlight. Show him how to direct the light, tracing the chalkboard number carefully.
3. Add more numbers when appropriate.

TEACHER-TO-TEACHER TIP
- For extra practice, give the children buckets of water and brushes to paint numbers on the sidewalk.

SONG
Trace This Line by Susan Oldham Hill
(Tune: "This Little Light of Mine")
This little line of mine,
I'm gonna trace this line.
I'm gonna trace this two,
See what I can do.
I'm gonna trace a three,
Just you wait and see!
Trace this line, trace this line, trace this line.

ASSESSMENT
To assess the children's learning, consider the following:
- Give the children markers and colorful paper. Show the children number cards. Can the children copy the numbers on their papers?
- Can each child trace the numbers on the chalkboard with the flashlight?

Susan Oldham Hill, Lakeland, FL

Children's Books

Anno's Counting House by Mitsumasa Anno
Count! by Denise Fleming
Moja Means One by Muriel Feelings
This Old Man by Tony Ross

Hidden Numbers

4+

LEARNING OBJECTIVES

The children will:
1. Learn about numbers 1–10.
2. See shapes in numbers.

Materials

black sketch pen
10" x 10" cards
envelopes
scissors (adult only)

VOCABULARY

curve	peek	slanting line	straight line
observe	shape	curving line	

PREPARATION

- Print out or write one digit on each card.
- Place the card inside the envelope.
- Cut a small hole on one side of the envelope such that only the middle portion of the number is visible.

WHAT TO DO

1. Hold the envelope high so that the children can see only the middle part of the number.
2. Let the children guess the number inside the envelope. If they run out of guesses, show them the number.

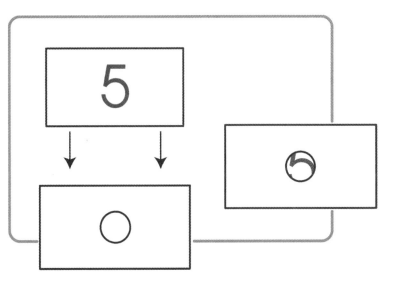

ASSESSMENT

To assess the children's learning, consider the following:
- Display the number card. Can the children identify the number?
- Can the children identify the lines in numbers, such as circles, curving lines, slanted lines, and straight lines?

Shyamala Shanmugasundaram, Nerul, Navi Mumbai, India

Children's Books

All About 1 2 3 by
Ruth Thomson
I Spy Little Numbers by
Jean Marzollo
*My Very First Book of
Numbers* by Eric Carle

Number Fun

4+

LEARNING OBJECTIVES

The children will:

1. Learn to count.
2. Learn to make sets that match a number.

Materials

number cards
small bag or box
small objects to
   count

VOCABULARY

group   number names   set

PREPARATION

● As an example for the children, make numbers cards that list the number and
   have the same number of dots as well.

WHAT TO DO

1. Ask a child to draw out a
   number card and name
   the number.
2. Ask the rest of the children
   to stand and find friends to
   make a set of people to
   match the number. For
   example, if a child draws a
   three, the children should
   get in groups of three.
   When they finish, go from
   group to group counting
   the sets with the children
   in each group.

3. Choose another child to draw out a different number card. Again, ask the
   children to make sets to match that number.

ASSESSMENT

To assess the children's learning, consider the following:

● Show the children several groups of small objects. Can each child accurately
   count the amount of objects?
● Give a child the number cards. Can the child put the cards in the correct
   order?

Susan Oldham Hill, Lakeland, FL

Children's Books

26 Letters and 99 Cents
   by Tana Hoban
Count and See by
   Tana Hoban
Moja Means One by
   Muriel Feelings
*One Child, One Seed:
   A South African
   Counting Book* by
   Kathryn Cave

Number Hero

LEARNING OBJECTIVES

The children will:
1. Identify numbers.
2. Recognize health and safety topics.
3. Improve language skills.

Materials

4" or larger plastic
   or card stock
   numbers
down vest
permanent marker,
   fabric paint, or
   number stickers
coat hook
"Number Hero"
   name card
colorful sand pail
   with a handle

VOCABULARY

cut	fall	injure	safe
danger	hurt	numbers	

PREPARATION

- Use the markers, fabric paint, or stickers to add numbers randomly on the down vest and the colorful sand pail.
- Hang the "Number Hero" name card above a coat hook. Hang the vest on the hook.
- Display the number cards randomly about the room in places that could be a safety hazard, such as on the stairs, on the edge of the sink, near a pair of scissors, and so on.

WHAT TO DO

1. Invite one child each day to be the class Number Hero.
2. Have the selected child put on the numbered vest and carry the numbered bucket.
3. Instruct the Number Hero to walk around the room and "rescue" one of the numbers from danger.
4. Each time the Number Hero picks up a number, he places it in the bucket and carries it back to the circle area. He then pours the number out on the floor and tells how he rescued that specific number from certain danger.
5. After all 10 numbers have been "rescued" the child hangs the vest and the pail back on the hook.
6. Children will look forward to rescuing the numbers on a daily basis.

ASSESSMENT

To assess the children's learning, consider the following:
- Can each child identify numbers and verbalize how they "rescued" each number from a dangerous situation?
- Do the children know safety rules? Can they describe one or more?

Mary J. Murray, Mazomanie, WI

Children's Books

The Balancing Act: A Counting Song by Merle Peek
Clothes by Fiona Pragoff
No Little Hippo by Jane Belk Moncure

Before and After

5+

LEARNING OBJECTIVES

The children will:

1. Learn to recognize numbers.
2. Learn where numbers come in the counting sequence.

Materials

9" x 12" tagboard
number cards
with large
numbers 1–10

VOCABULARY

clue   riddle

WHAT TO DO

1. Arrange the cards 1–5 on the chalk rail or on the rug so all the children can see them.
2. Point to each card, asking the children to name the number.
3. Ask the children the following questions. Choose one child to point to the correct card and name the number.

   Questions for cards 1–5:
   * I come after 4. What number am I?
   * I come before 2. What number am I?

4. Continue with these riddles, giving the clue and asking, What number am I?:
   * I come after 3.
   * I come before 5.
   * I come after 1.
   * I come before 4.
   * I come after 2.
   * I come before 3.

5. When the children are successful with 1–5, add 6–10 to the lineup, using these clues:
   * I come after 6.
   * I come before 8.
   * I come after 7.
   * I come before 9.
   * I come after 8.
   * I come after 9.
   * I come before 10.
   * I come before 7.

ASSESSMENT

To assess the children's learning, consider the following:
* Give the children number cards 1–5 in random order. Can the children put the cards in the correct order?
* Can the children answer the number questions easily?

Children's Books

Count! by
Denise Fleming
Moja Means One by
Muriel Feelings
*One Child, One Seed:
A South African
Counting Book* by
Kathryn Cave

Susan Oldham Hill, Lakeland, FL

Handprint Number Chart 5+

LEARNING OBJECTIVES

The children will:
1. Learn to count.
2. Learn to recognize numbers.

VOCABULARY

column   handprint   number names 1–10

PREPARATION

- Make a grid from bulletin board paper with 10 rows and 12 columns with 6″ squares.
- In the first column on the left side, write numbers 1–10.
- Spread newspaper to cover the surface and floor area.

WHAT TO DO

1. Spread the grid out on the rug or tack it to a bulletin board.
2. Ask a child to read the first number on the first row (one). Ask how many handprints should go on this row (one).
3. Ask the children, "How many more handprints should go on this row?" If they can't tell you, explain that no more handprints should go there, because the number 1 means one handprint.
4. Ask another child to read the number in the next row (two), and ask her to tell you how many handprints should go on that row. Paint the child's hand with the color of her choice, and press it carefully in the square next to the number two.
5. Continue until all the numbers have the correct number of handprints.
6. Extend the children's learning by talking about the chart. Ask a child to point to a number and choose that number of friends to hold hands.
7. Display the chart on a bulletin board or wall.

ASSESSMENT

To assess the children's learning, consider the following:
- Do the children understand the concept of zero?
- Can the children count all of the handprints on the chart?

Susan Oldham Hill, Lakeland, FL

Children's Books

Hand Rhymes by Marc Brown
How Do Dinosaurs Count to Ten? by Jane Yolen
My Five Senses by Aliki

Number Necklaces

5+

LEARNING OBJECTIVES

The children will:

1. Learn to recognize numbers.
2. Learn to put numbers in order.

Materials

markers
10 tagboard cards,
  5" x 7"
yarn
scissors (adult only)
hole punch

VOCABULARY

number   order   sequence

PREPARATION

● Make number cards with the 5" x 7" tagboard cards, writing one number
  from 1–10 on each card. Punch two holes in the top edge of each card.
  Thread and tie lengths of yarn through the holes, creating number necklaces
  that can easily fit over a child's head.

WHAT TO DO

1. Show the number card necklaces to the children in random order, asking them
   to name each one. Practice several times.
2. Put them in the correct order, and ask the children to name them again.
3. Next, mix up the order and give them to 10 children to put on. Ask them to
   stand in front of the group.
4. Tell the children that the numbers are all mixed up, and ask one child to find
   the number that should come first in the line.
5. When someone has found the child wearing the "one" necklace, ask that child
   to stand at the left side of the line. Continue looking for the "two" necklace,
   and continue until they are all in sequence.

TEACHER-TO-TEACHER TIP

● To help the children, have an extra set of cards in order on the floor, so they
  can compare the right sequence of the numbers.

ASSESSMENT

To assess the children's learning, consider the following:

● Can each child name the numbers in random order?
● Can each child put the number cards in order?

Susan Oldham Hill, Lakeland, FL

Children's Books

1 Is One by
Tasha Tudor
Count! by
Denise Fleming
Moja Means One by
Muriel Feelings
*One Potato: A Counting
Book of Potato Prints* by
Diana Pomeroy
This Old Man by
Tony Ross

Today's Number Is...

5+

LEARNING OBJECTIVES

The children will:

1. Develop cognitive (logical) thinking by using numbers and counting.
2. Develop language, listening, and speaking skills by understanding and following verbal instruction.

Materials

set of cardboard
  number pieces
  with big black
  numbers on
  them from 1–10
  (or 20)
several small toys
  (plastic animals
  or cars)
bag
box

VOCABULARY

abacus   even   odd   zero
dozen

PREPARATION

● Place number cards in a bag and a variety of small toys in a box.

WHAT TO DO

1. Have a special "number time" once a week. Designate a different child each week to be the special person in charge of the weekly number.
2. Start "number time" with the following number song:

   The Number Song by Freya Zellerhoff
   (Tune: "Do You Know the Muffin Man?")
   Do you know what time it is?   *Do you know what time it is?*
   What time it is, what time it is?   *It's time to learn our number!*

3. Blindfold the designated child or ask him to close his eyes. Let the child pick a number without looking, so it will be a surprise.
4. Announce the number of the day to everyone: "And today's number is ____!"
5. The designated child picks as many plastic animals (or other toys) as the day's special number calls for. The child arranges the animals or toys on a special display area (a shelf or a desk).

TEACHER-TO-TEACHER TIP

● For advanced classes, have the children group the plastic animals by twos or fives.

Children's Books

The Baker's Dozen: A Counting Book by Dan Andreasen
One Hundred Hungry Ants by Elinor Pinczes
Ten Little Ladybugs by Melanie Gerth

ASSESSMENT

To assess the children's learning, consider the following:

● Can the children recognize the number and count up to that number?
● Can the children count and group items by twos or fives?
● Are the children's conversations improving?

Freya Zellerhoff, Towson, MD

Cooking with Numbers

3+

LEARNING OBJECTIVES

The children will:
1. Identify numbers.
2. Improve their oral language skills.
3. Improve their social skills.

Materials

plastic numbers
toy or real cooking
   materials such as
   pots, pans,
   bowls, plates,
   muffin tins,
   baking pans
spatulas and
   spoons
pot holders
children's oven or
   stove

VOCABULARY

bake	flip	mix	stir
cook	fry		

WHAT TO DO

1. Place the materials at the dramatic play center.
2. Invite the children to cook, bake, fry, mix, stir, and serve up a platter of numbers.
3. Allow the children to serve numbers to their classmates on plates and in bowls.
4. Invite the children to talk about the numbers as they work at the dramatic play center.

TEACHER-TO-TEACHER TIP

- If you do not have a child's oven or stove, simply draw the outline of burners and an oven door on an inverted cardboard box to create your own stove.

ASSESSMENT

To assess the children's learning, consider the following:
- Ask the children to place a spatula full of numbers onto a plate. Can the children identify each number served?
- Pass a large bowl of numbers and a mixing spoon around the circle of children. Can each child name one or more of the numbers in the bowl?
- Tape a number card to each kitchen item from the learning center. Can the children identify the numbers on the kitchen utensils and cookware?

Mary J. Murray, Mazomanie, WI

Children's Books

Eating the Alphabet by
   Lois Ehlert
Food for Thought by
   Saxton Freymann
I Want to Be a Chef by
   Stephanie Maze

Number Picnic

4+

LEARNING OBJECTIVES

The children will:
1. Improve their social skills.
2. Improve their number-recognition skills.

Materials

twin bed sheet in a solid color
fabric paints or permanent marker
20 or more colorful plastic or card stock numbers stored in a plastic container
picnic supplies such as plates, bowls, cups, napkins, plastic straws, and plastic silverware
picnic basket

VOCABULARY

| basket | bowl | eat | plate |
| blanket | cup | picnic | silverware |

PREPARATION

- Use the fabric paints or markers to write numbers randomly on the sheet. Let dry.
- Place the materials inside the picnic basket.

WHAT TO DO

1. Invite two or more children to carry the picnic basket to an open area of the classroom.
2. Ask the children to spread out the number blanket and set the picnic basket in the middle.
3. Encourage the children to remove the tableware from the basket and place the items on the blanket, getting ready for a picnic.
4. Suggest that the children remove the numbers from the container and place several on the plates, in the bowls, and in the cups.
5. Invite the children to role-play a picnic as they identify and enjoy a number picnic.
6. After the children have explored the numbers and the picnic materials, challenge them to identify numbers on the blanket.

TEACHER-TO-TEACHER TIP

- Remind the children not to let their drinking cups, silverware, or any other items touch their mouths.

Children's Books

Picnic Pandemonium by Christina M. Butler
Teddy Bears' Picnic by Jimmy Kennedy
Winter Picnic by Robert Welber

ASSESSMENT

To assess the children's learning, consider the following:
- Can each child name the numbers on her plate and in her cup?
- Hand a paper plate to each child in the class. Provide each child with a handful of plastic or card stock numbers. Can each child name the numbers on her plate?

Mary J. Murray, Mazomanie, WI

Number Puppets

4+

LEARNING OBJECTIVES

The children will:
1. Improve their oral-language skills.
2. Develop their number-recognition skills.
3. Develop their social skills.

Materials

puppets (10 if
   possible)
number cards
safety pins or yarn
   and paper
   punch
large cardboard
   box or puppet
   theatre
number chart

VOCABULARY

hand	puppet	speak	talk
numbers			

PREPARATION

- Pin or tie one number card to the front of each puppet.
- Display the box on a table.
- Display the puppets and number chart near the box.

WHAT TO DO

1. Invite small groups of children to select a puppet and put on a puppet show for a group of their classmates.
2. Children can sit behind the box as they manipulate the puppets.
3. Invite the puppets to talk with one another about their numbers and refer to the number chart in their conversations.
4. Encourage the children to use their puppets to count objects or describe the number they hold.
5. When the first group is finished, the children in the audience can applaud after which another small group of children can put on another puppet show.

TEACHER-TO-TEACHER TIP

- If you do not have puppets, make simple sock puppets. Use permanent markers to add two eyes to each sock, then attach the number card and proceed as directed above.

ASSESSMENT

To assess the children's learning, consider the following:
- Display the number chart. Can each child manipulate a puppet as she identifies each number on the chart?
- Can the children describe the numbers once they identify them?

Mary J. Murray, Mazomanie, WI

Children's Books

My Numbers by
Neil Ricklen
Numbers by
Melanie Watt
*Ten What? A Mystery
Counting Book* by
Russell Hoban

Let's Keep Score

3+

LEARNING OBJECTIVES

The children will:

1. Participate in cooperative behavior.
2. Exercise motor skills and be able to toss the beanbag accurately at the target.
3. Begin to learn about scores.

Materials

socks or knee-high nylons
beans or corn
chalk, masking tape, or washable paint

PREPARATION

- Help the children make three beanbags by filling socks or nylons with beans or corn.
- Draw a circular "bull's eye" target on the ground (with chalk, masking tape, or washable paint). Start with three concentric circles, making the outside circle 6' across.
- In the middle circle write the number 3. Inside the second circle write the number 2. Inside the outside circle write the number 1. Mark a "start" line so the children know where to stand when throwing the beanbags.

WHAT TO DO

1. Explain to the children that they will take turns throwing three beanbags into the target. Explain that the middle circle earns them the most points. Initially, you will want to help them add up their points.
2. Record the children's points on a chart.
3. As the children become more adept at the game, challenge them to record their scores on the chart themselves.
4. Consider extending this activity by moving the "start" line farther away from the target. Or, you may add more circles to the target, maybe starting with five in the middle.

ASSESSMENT

To assess the children's learning, consider the following:

- Can each child toss the beanbag accurately?
- Can each child add?
- Is the child ready to move on to more advanced counting and adding?

Judy Fujawa, The Villages, FL

Children's Books

Numbers and Sports by J. M. Patton
Ten What? A Mystery Counting Book by Russell Hoban

Two Hands, One Heart

LEARNING OBJECTIVES

The children will:

1. Review the numbers one and two.
2. Learn about the body.

Materials

anatomical poster
or chart
(optional)

VOCABULARY

ankles	cheeks	forehead	mouth	throat
arms	chest	hands	neck	thumbs
backbone/	chin	head	nose	tummy/
spine	ears	heels	scalp	abdomen
body	elbows	hips	shins	wrists
bottom	eyebrows	jaw	shoulders	
calves	feet	knees	thighs	

WHAT TO DO

1. Display an anatomical chart if possible. Children love the details and textures on charts designed for adults.
2. Ask the children to stand up. Point to your nose and say, "One nose." Ask the children to do the same.
3. Now hold your earlobes and say, "two ears."
4. Continue touching and naming singular and plural body parts while the children repeat what you say.
5. End by pressing your two hands over your one heart.

TEACHER-TO-TEACHER TIP

- You can adjust the vocabulary according to the age and ability of the children, and go through as many or as few parts as they will follow. Make the activity more dynamic by increasing the speed and the distance between parts (for example, "One neck! Two ankles!"). You could also simply point to a given body part or pair of body parts for the children to name.

ASSESSMENT

To assess the children's learning, consider the following:

- Can the children count the number of elbows, arms, hands, they have?
- Can the children add the number of hands they have to the number of arms they have? Challenge them to add together the numbers of other body parts they have, or to break into pairs and add their body parts together.

Patrick Mitchell, Yagoto, Nagoya, Japan

Children's Books

From Head to Toe by
Eric Carle
*I Love You with All My
Heart* by Noris Kern
My Day with Numbers
by Christine Powers

Song

"Head, Shoulders,
Knees, and Toes"

Beat the Clock

4+

LEARNING OBJECTIVES

The children will:

1. Develop physical coordination and class cooperation.
2. Reinforce counting from 1–10.

Materials

digital timer
wooden blocks
chalk and chalk
board or marker
and chart paper

VOCABULARY

| finish | start | timer | transportation |
hand to hand

WHAT TO DO

1. Line the children up from one end of the classroom to the other. Ask the children, "How long will it take you to pass this block from start to finish?" After they answer, say, "Let's use a timer and find out!"
2. Hand the block to the first child as you start the timer and say, "Go."
3. The children pass the block from hand to hand. The last child drops the block in a basket to stop the timer.
4. Show the children the numbers on the timer and write this number on a chalk board or chart paper. Then ask them if they can move the next block faster!
5. After the group is working together smoothly, help the children count out a set of up to 10 blocks. They can time their movement of the whole set of blocks, and then try again to beat the clock.

TEACHER-TO-TEACHER TIPS

● This activity is best when the children are feeling alert and energetic. Other objects such as plush toys or plastic eggs on spoons could also be used.
● The children will discover the need for teamwork. Without the cooperation of every link in the chain, they won't be able to beat the clock.

ASSESSMENT

To assess the children's learning, consider the following:
● Do the children work well as a team?
● Can the children pass the block to one another without dropping it?

Patrick Mitchell, Yagoto, Nagoya, Japan

Children's Books

Clickety Clack by Rob Spence and Amy Spence
Freight Train by Donald Crews
How Do Dinosaurs Count to Ten? by Jane Yolen

Clapping Game

4+

LEARNING OBJECTIVES

The children will:

1. Recognize numbers 0–5 and, eventually, 0–10.
2. Associate quantity to numbers.
3. Increase their attention span.

Materials

wooden cube

VOCABULARY

body parts	clap	number names	stamp
(hands, feet,	cube		
tongue)			

PREPARATION

● Write the numbers 0–5 on the six faces of the cube. You may prepare a second cube (0, 6, 7, 8, 9, and 10) once the children master the first one.

WHAT TO DO

1. Ask the children to sit in a circle. They take turns rolling the cube. When the cube stops, the number on top indicates how many times they should clap.
   Note: Explain to the children that when the cube lands on 0, they should not clap at all.
2. For variety, have the children snap their fingers, click their tongues, or stand and stamp their feet. This is a good way to teach the concept of zero, so be sure 0 is on each cube.

ASSESSMENT

To assess the children's learning, consider the following:

● Can the children recognize the numbers?
● Can the children clap the appropriate number of times?
● Can the children begin to understand the concept of zero?

Mary Jo Shannon, Roanoke, VA

Children's Books

All About 1 2 3 by Ruth Thomson
Count! by Denise Fleming
Count and See by Tana Hoban

Song and Fingerplay

"If You're Happy and You Know It"
"Five Little Monkeys Jumping on the Bed"

Count Them Out!

4+

LEARNING OBJECTIVES

The children will:

1. Learn to recognize the numbers 1–10.
2. Learn to count to 10.

two bags
two sets of number
cards 1–10

VOCABULARY

captain	line	shout
count	number names	team

PREPARATION

- Place one set of number cards in each bag, creating two bags of number cards.

WHAT TO DO

1. Take the children outside and divide them into two teams. Ask the children to stand in a line behind their captain.
2. The first team chants the following:

   Hear Me Shout by Susan Oldham Hill
   Hear me shout!
   Hear me shout!
   Choose a number
   And count it out!

3. After the chant, team two draws a card from their bag of number cards. If the number is three, for example, the captain counts the first child in line, saying the numbers one, two, and three while counting them. These three children then go to the end of the line and sit down. The captain would also go to the end of the line and sit down. The number one child becomes the new captain.
4. Team two chants the rhyme above. Team one draws a card from their bag, and the captain counts that number of children, who sit down. The captain sits at the end of the line, and the number one child becomes the new captain.
5. Continue until all children are seated, and start over if time allows.

ASSESSMENT

To assess the children's learning, consider the following:

- Give one child 10 items. Can he count the items?
- Show each child number cards. Can he identify all the numbers?

Children's Books

Count! by
Denise Fleming
How Many Snails? by
Paul Giganti, Jr.
*Knots on a Counting
Rope* by Bill Martin, Jr.
Moja Means One by
Muriel Feelings

Susan Oldham Hill, Lakeland, FL

Mail Delivery

LEARNING OBJECTIVES

The children will:
1. Learn number recognition.
2. Learn matching.

Materials

poster board
small envelopes
construction paper
stapler
scissors (adult only)

VOCABULARY

delivery   mail   mail carrier   matching

PREPARATION

● Draw five houses on the poster board.
● Cut sheets of construction paper in half.
● Staple the half sheets onto the poster board under each house; this will form the pockets in which the children will need to place the envelopes.
● Write a number from 1–5 on each of the houses and the envelopes.
● If you wish, cover the board with contact paper or laminate it so it will last longer.

WHAT TO DO

1. When the children come over to play the game, explain to them that they will be mail carriers and deliver the mail to each house.
2. Show the children the envelopes and explain that the number on each of the envelopes corresponds to a number on the house.
3. When the children find the houses that match their numbers, they can put the correct envelope in the pocket below the house.

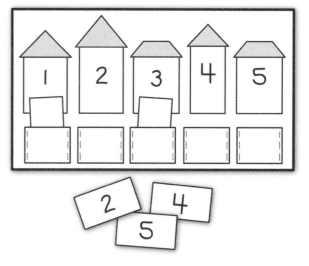

ASSESSMENT

To assess the children's learning, consider the following:
● Do the children recognize the numbers on the envelopes?
● As the children play the game, can they match the number on the envelope to the correct house?

Children's Books

Here Comes Mr. Eventoff with the Mail by Alice K. Flanagan
The Post Office Book: Mail and How It Moves by Gail Gibbons
Will Goes to the Post Office by Olof Landstrom

Sherri Lawrence, Louisville, KY

Number Dash

LEARNING OBJECTIVES

The children will:
1. Participate in large motor play.
2. Identify numbers by appearance.
3. Experience organized game play and rules.

Materials

sidewalk chalk
large paved area

VOCABULARY

dash   number names

PREPARATION

● Write large numbers in various spots on the paved area. Be sure that there is one of each number for each child.

WHAT TO DO

1. Explain to the children that you will call out a number. When they hear it, they need to dash to one of those numbers and stand on it. But they must wait and not move until you call the number.

2. Ask the children who have found a number to cheer on and assist those who are still looking.
3. Encourage the children to take turns shouting numbers.

TEACHER-TO-TEACHER TIPS

● Use dark chalk colors on light pavement, and vice versa for dark pavement.
● Spread the numbers out sufficiently so children won't collide. You can also play this game with shapes, letters, or colors.

Children's Books

Boom Chicka Rock by John Archambault
Counting Crocodiles by Judy Sierra
The Counting Race by Margaret McNamara

ASSESSMENT

To assess the children's learning, consider the following:
● Can the children find the numbers with little assistance?
● Can the children follow the rules with minimal reminders?

Jaclyn Miller, Mishawaka, IN

Number Hunt

LEARNING OBJECTIVES

The children will:

1. Recognize number names and numbers by sight.
2. Learn to put numbers in order.

Materials

cards, books, or pictures that show a number name or numbers big enough to be easily recognized by the children (if unavailable, draw on a blackboard or place brightly colored handmade number cards around the room)

VOCABULARY

number names   order   scavenger hunt

PREPARATION

- Before the children enter the room, place number names and numbers around the room. Hiding some inside desks or cubbies and playing "Hot and Cold" are fun too.

WHAT TO DO

1. Explain to the children they are going on a "scavenger hunt" to find number names and numbers.
   Note: Children can hunt individually or in teams. Teams usually work well.
2. Children should find all the cards, pictures, and so on, from 1–10.
3. Give hints if some of the cards are well hidden.
4. Provide a place where children can line up the numbers and number names in order.

TEACHER-TO-TEACHER TIP

- It's fun to do this within a certain amount of time. Children love to beat the clock. It's also best to use only one set of numbers or number names per team. Or, try designating a day of all "ones" or "twos."

ASSESSMENT

To assess the children's learning, consider the following:

- Can the children recognize numbers and number names by sight?
- Can the children line up the numbers in order from 1–10?

Donna Alice Patton, Hillsboro, OH

Children's Books

How Do Dinosaurs Count to Ten by Jane Yolen
My One Book by Jane Belk Moncure (This is a series that goes to *My Ten Book*.)
Ten Black Dots by Donald Crews

Numberpillar

4+

LEARNING OBJECTIVES

The children will:
1. Complete a caterpillar puzzle.
2. Place numbers in numerical sequence from 1–10.
3. Recognize numbers 1–10.

Materials

poster board in
various colors,
including black
scissors (adult only)
markers

VOCABULARY

antennae	number	numerical order	sequence
caterpillar	number names		

PREPARATION

- Cut out 10–15 large circles from the poster board, and one extra for the head. Vary the colors.
- Use black poster board to make legs for each circle and antennae for the head.
- Decorate the head with eyes, a nose, and a mouth, and attach antennae. Attach the legs to each circle.
- Write one number from 1–10 on each circle, except the head.
- If possible, laminate the pieces for durability.

WHAT TO DO

1. Show the children the caterpillar pieces.
2. Hand out the numbered circles and talk about the numbers on the circles and see if the children can name the numbers they have. See if they can guess what animal this is supposed to be.
3. Tell the children that this caterpillar has to get ready for school, but he needs to put his colors on in numerical order.
4. Place the head on the floor and ask the children what number comes first when you count. See if they can find who has number one.
5. That child can come up and attach his circle onto the head. Continue finding numbers in numerical order until the whole caterpillar is complete.
6. Leave the game in the math area for the children to complete independently.

Children's Books

Counting Colors by Roger Priddy
Fun with Counting by Jenny Ackland
The Very Hungry Caterpillar by Eric Carle

ASSESSMENT

To assess the children's learning, consider the following:
- Can the children complete this puzzle independently?
- Can the children put the numbers 1–10 in the correct order using other materials?

Shelley Hoster, Norcross, GA

Number Shopping

4+

LEARNING OBJECTIVES

The children will:

1. Identify numbers.
2. Identify food items.
3. Improve social skills.

Materials

four brown grocery
bags
10 or more various
food containers
per bag, total of
40
colorful number
cards or number
stickers

VOCABULARY

bags   groceries   numbers   shopping
carry

PREPARATION

● Attach a colored number card or number sticker to each food container.
● Place an assortment of containers in each grocery bag.

WHAT TO DO

1. Invite a group of four children to work at the dramatic play center for this game.
2. Encourage each child to pick up a grocery bag and carry it around the room.
3. Have the children return to the "play house" area, pretending to come home from a grocery shopping trip.
4. Invite the children to take turns as they remove items from their bags and identify the number on each item.
5. Allow the children to work until all the items are displayed at the center and they have identified each number.
6. Invite the children to return 10 items to the bags so the game is ready for the next set of children.

ASSESSMENT

To assess the children's learning, consider the following:

● Ask one child to select an item from a grocery bag. Can the child name the number on the item and then display it on the table?
● Sit with the children. Have each child hold a bag of numbered groceries. Invite the children to take turns removing items from their bags. Can each child identify all the numbers in his bag?

Mary J. Murray, Mazomanie, WI

Children's Books

26 Letters and 99 Cents
by Tana Hoban
*A Busy Day at Mr.
Kang's Grocery Store* by
Alice Flanagan
*Jonathan Goes to the
Grocery Store* by
Susan K. Baggette
*What's It Like to Be a
Grocer?* by
Shelley Wilks

Tap a Number

4+

LEARNING OBJECTIVES
The children will:
1. Identify numbers and count 1–10.
2. Learn to concentrate and improve their listening skills.

Materials

index cards
pen
box

VOCABULARY

count   door   knock   pound

PREPARATION
● Write a different number on
  each card and put the cards
  in a box.

WHAT TO DO
1. Let a child pick up a card
   from the box and stand
   outside the door of the room.
2. Ask the child to knock on the
   door as many times as the
   number written on the card.
3. The other children sitting
   inside the classroom have to
   listen and tell how many
   times the child knocked.
4. Let the other children take
   turns knocking.

ASSESSMENT
To assess the children's learning, consider the following:
● Can the children count their fingers in ascending order?
● Can the children identify the numbers written on the cards?

Shyamala Shanmugasundaram, Nerul, Navi Mumbai, India

Children's Books

All About 1 2 3 by
Ruth Thomson
Anno's Counting House
by Mitsumasa Anno
*My Very First Book of
Numbers* by Eric Carle

Catch the Number

LEARNING OBJECTIVES

The children will:

1. Model addition (joining) and subtraction (separating).
2. Relate everyday language to mathematical language and symbols.

Materials

beach ball with colored sections
permanent marker

VOCABULARY

addition   catch   hold   subtraction

PREPARATION

● Write the numbers 1–9 in the colored sections of the beach ball. Spread them over the entire ball. Repeat numbers.

WHAT TO DO

1. With the children, review safety rules for tossing a beach ball in class and discuss the potential for someone to get hurt if they do not follow the rules.
2. Work with a small group of children. Have one child toss the ball to a friend. When he catches the ball, he looks at the numbers his thumbs are touching. Ask the child to read the numbers aloud. Then he tosses the ball to the next friend.
3. If the child is not sure of the numbers, he can use class resources, refer to a number line, or ask a friend for help.
4. To create some differentiation for children that need a challenge, when the child holds the ball, ask him to add or subtract the numbers his thumbs are on.
5. Encourage each child to say the equation aloud to help work through it. "My thumbs are on two and four. So, two plus four equals six."
6. Place the ball back in the math center when the game is over.

ASSESSMENT

To assess the children's learning, consider the following:

● How well did the children use language during the game?
● Did the children use teamwork when passing the ball?
● Can the children create and solve number sentences?

Sunny Hyde, Austin, TX

Children's Books

Count! by Denise Fleming
Ten Black Dots by Donald Crews
Twelve Days of Kindergarten: A Counting Book by Deborah Lee Rose

Kite Numbers

5+

LEARNING OBJECTIVES

The children will:
1. Make a kite.
2. Print numbers on a kite.
3. Play a kite action game.

Materials

white construction
   paper 8½″ x 11″
felt pens
scissors (adult only)
string
hole punch
ribbons
crayons

VOCABULARY

kite   number   ribbon   string

PREPARATION

- Use a black felt pen to outline a kite on construction paper. Photocopy enough kites for the class. Precut string for the kites about 6″.

WHAT TO DO

1. Give each child a paper kite. Ask them to cut out the kite.
2. Ask the children to punch a hole in their kites, for the tail.
3. Ask the children to color their kites, and to print a number on the kite. Say, "Choose a number between one and five. Place one of these numbers on your kite. We are going to play a kite number game." Then help the children to print their names at the bottom of their kites.
4. Ask the group of children to hold up their kites. Play a version of "Simon Says" by giving the children directions, such as:
   - If you have a number five on your kite, stretch to the sky.
   - If you have a number two on your kite, jump up and down.
   - If you have a number three on your kite, run in place.
   - If you have a number one on your kite, turn around in circles.
   - If you have a number four on your kite, hop around.

ASSESSMENT

To assess the children's learning, consider the following:
- Display the kites in class. Can each child tell you about his kite? Listen to all the children's comments. Write down their comments if possible.
- Can the children tell you how many numbers they saw today?

> Lily Erlic, Victoria, British Columbia, Canada

Children's Books

Count! by
Denise Fleming
Curious George Flies a Kite by H. A. Rey
Let's Fly a Kite by
Stuart J. Murphy

Teacher, May I?

5+

LEARNING OBJECTIVES

The children will:
1. Practice counting.
2. Identify numbers.
3. Follow simple rules.
4. Practice large motor skills.

Materials

10 pieces of card
   stock (8½" x 11")
dark marker or
   paint

VOCABULARY

| hop | number names | skip | step |
| jump | | | |

PREPARATION

- Make number cards for numbers 1–10 using the card stock and a dark marker or paint. On each piece of card stock, write one of the numbers. Each number should fill up most of the page and be easy to read from far away.

WHAT TO DO

1. Have the children stand shoulder to shoulder in a line on one side of an open area.
2. Stand at the other end of the open area with the number cards.
3. Taking turns, have the children request to move toward you. They should ask, "Teacher, may I hop?" They can request to step, hop, jump, skip, and so on.
4. Reply to the child by holding up a number card, but don't read the number. "You may hop [hold up a number card] times."
5. Have the child reply, identifying the number. "Teacher, I will hop five times." The child takes five hops toward you.
6. Continue playing until the children reach you.

TEACHER-TO-TEACHER TIP

- To make this activity easier for children who are not yet able to recognize written numbers, say the number while holding up the number card. This will help the children associate the written number with the spoken number.

ASSESSMENT

To assess the children's learning, consider the following:
- Can each child identify and name the number?
- Can each child count to the specified number?
- Can each child perform the specified task?

Children's Books

*1-2-3: A Child's First
Counting Book* by
Alison Jay
Counting Colors by
Roger Priddy
Numbers by
Melanie Watt

Janet Hammond, Mount Laurel, NJ

Triple Match

5+

LEARNING OBJECTIVES

The children will:

1. Learn to see numbers three ways.
2. Recognize the sameness of numbers no matter how they write them.
3. Write and recognize number names.
4. Use small motor skills to create a game.

Materials

30 index cards per
  child
newspaper
shirt or smock per
  child
markers, crayons,
  or colored
  pencils
nontoxic paint
hand wipes

VOCABULARY

amount   number words   same

PREPARATION

- Have each child bring in a pack of blank index cards. White is best; colored cards can be distracting.
- Spread newspaper and create a painting area before the children arrive.

WHAT TO DO

1. To make number cards, ask the children to take 10 cards and, holding the cards vertically, help them write one number per card from 1–10 using different colors.
2. Ask the children to take 10 cards and help them write number words ("one," "two," "three," and so on), one per card, from 1–10. Challenge the children to match the number color from the first cards.
3. To make the counting cards, the children take the last 10 cards, dip a thumb or finger into the paint, and make the correct number of dots to match each number. Let these dry overnight.
4. Younger children may need assistance matching colors across all three types of cards.
5. When all the cards are ready, play "Triple Match."
6. Lay cards face down and try to find matches three ways: "one," "1," and one painted dot.

ASSESSMENT

To assess the children's learning, consider the following:

- Can the children recognize the numbers?
- Do the children understand that numbers never change no matter how they are written?

Donna Alice Patton, Hillsboro, OH

Children's Books

Count and See by
Tana Hoban
Ten Black Dots by
Donald Crews
*The Crayon Counting
Book* by Pam Munoz
Ryan and Jerry Pallotta

Purse Full of Number Fun 3+

LEARNING OBJECTIVES

The children will:
1. Identify numbers.
2. Develop oral language skills.
3. Improve social skills.

Materials

two purses
(preferably that
open and close
with a clasp)
plastic numbers or
numbers cut
from colorful
card stock

VOCABULARY

buy   open   purse   spend
numbers

PREPARATION

- Place five numbers inside each purse and shut it.

WHAT TO DO

1. Ask two children to open the purses.
2. Invite the children to peek at the numbers inside and identify them silently.
3. Have the two children take turns removing a number from the purse and using the number in a sentence, such as "I'm going to buy two apples," or "I'm going to spend five dollars on lunch."
4. After all five numbers have been removed from each purse, have the children place the numbers back inside for the next pair of players.

TEACHER-TO-TEACHER TIP

- Purchase an assortment of fun and fancy purses at rummage sales or second-hand shops. Consider purchasing several wallets as well. Place an assortment of colorful paper or card stock number cards inside each wallet. Use the wallets in the same way the purses were used.

ASSESSMENT

To assess the children's learning, consider the following:
- Listen to each pair of children as they play the game. Evaluate their number recognition and language skills.
- Display an assortment of number cards before the class. Can the children match the numbers from the purse with the numbers on display?

Mary J. Murray, Mazomanie, WI

Children's Books

Lilly's Purple Plastic Purse by Kevin Henkes
Mad About Plaid by Jill McElmurry
Mouse Count by Ellen Stoll Walsh

Mystery Box

LEARNING OBJECTIVES

The children will:

1. Feel the shapes of numbers in the box.
2. Describe the shapes of the numbers, counting the number of sides, and describing lines as straight or curved.
3. Guess the name of the number, becoming progressively more accurate.

Materials

shoebox
large rubber or
   wooden
   numbers from
   1–9

VOCABULARY

number names   shape names

PREPARATION

- Cut a hole in one end of the shoebox big enough for a child to put her hand inside and handle the object in the box.

WHAT TO DO

1. Show the numbers to the children.
2. Ask the children to tell you the names of the numbers; if they do not know, tell them the names.
3. Talk about the shapes of the numbers—the straight parts and curved parts.
4. Without letting the children see, put one of the numbers in the box.
5. Let a child put her hand in the box and describe what she feels, and ask her to name the number.
6. Continue with other children until they name all the numbers in the box.

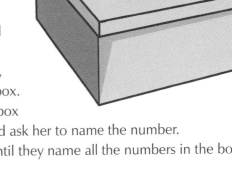

ASSESSMENT

To assess the children's learning, consider the following:

- Can the children identify which parts of the numbers are straight or curved?
- Can the children write the numbers as an extension to the activity?

Toni Rhodes, Stone Mountain, GA

Children's Books

Shape by Henry
Arthur Pluckrose
Size by Henry
Arthur Pluckrose
Spot's Colors, Shapes, and Numbers by
Eric Hill

Beanbag Toss

3+

LEARNING OBJECTIVES

The children will:
1. Throw a beanbag at a numbered target.
2. Begin to recognize the numbers 1–5.

Materials

stencils
markers
construction paper
masking tape
beanbags

VOCABULARY

| four | less | number names | throw |
| five | more | 1–5 | toss |

PREPARATION

- Trace around stencils of large numbers 1–5 onto construction paper. Use markers to fill in each number.
- Tape off a ladder-like shape or grid on the floor with five sections.
- Tape the numbers in ascending order inside the squares.
- Place the beanbags near the floor grid.

WHAT TO DO

1. Gather the children and tell them to look at the floor. Call their attention to the numbers inside the squares and see if they can name them.
2. Tell the children that they are going to learn their numbers in a fun way with the beanbags. Show them how to throw the beanbag into one of the numbered squares.
3. Give the first child a beanbag and see how far he can throw it. Have him call out the number on which his bag lands, hop from number to number, retrieve the beanbag, and hop back.
4. The children take turns doing this until every child has had a turn.
5. If you would like, you can make a graph on chart paper and write down the number that each child gets on his turn, like a scoreboard so the children can see you write the numbers that they are seeing on the floor.

TEACHER-TO-TEACHER TIP

- Make this game more challenging by adding more numbers and making the grid larger. Older children can begin to add up their own scores on chart paper.

ASSESSMENT

To assess the children's learning, consider the following:
- Does the child count using the correct number names?
- Can the child name a given number?
- Can the child throw the beanbag with consistent accuracy?

Children's Books

12 Ways to Get to 11 by Eve Merriam
Jump Frog Jump by Robert Kalan
Numbers by Melanie Watt

Shelley Hoster, Norcross, GA

Jumping Leaf Fun

3+

LEARNING OBJECTIVES

The children will:

1. Learn to count by jumping in the leaf heaps.
2. Learn vocabulary words to count their body parts.

Materials

several large bags
of dry leaves

VOCABULARY

arm	high	land	over
big	hip	leg	quick
crouch	jump	little	slow
foot	knee	low	under

PREPARATION

- Make large piles of leaves outdoors for the children to play in.
- Tell the children about how fun it can be to jump in piles of leaves.

WHAT TO DO

1. Show the children the piles of leaves.
2. Challenge them to jump in while using the vocabulary words to describe their jumping, such as *high*, *low*, or *crouch*.
3. Ask the children to count the number of times they can jump on the heap before it starts to go flat.
4. Ask the children to count how many times they can jump high, low, over, and under, and encourage the children to bend the different parts of their body and count the parts they are using.

TEACHER-TO-TEACHER TIP

- Be sure the children take turns and wait for one another to leave the heap before the next child jumps. This is a very exciting activity, but safety has to come first. Sometimes children will want to go under the leaves. This is fine, but be sure to supervise the children at all times.

ASSESSMENT

To assess the children's learning, consider the following:

- Can the children tell you how many times they landed on the heap of leaves?
- Can the children tell you how many times they jumped high?

Eileen Lucas, Fort McMurray, Alberta, Canada

Children's Books

All About 123 by
Ruth Thomson
A Frog in a Bog by
Karma Wilson
Ten, Nine, Eight by
Molly Bang

Leap Frog

3+

LEARNING OBJECTIVES
The children will:
1. Use their large muscles to jump on lily pads.
2. Read numbers as they jump.
3. Count as they jump.

Materials

blue plastic tarp or
large tablecloth
5–10 hula hoops
green butcher
paper or poster
board (optional)
construction paper
or poster board
tape
large open space
for pond

VOCABULARY

| count | jump | lily pad | pond |
| frog | leap | number names | |

PREPARATION
- Spread out the blue tarp (the "pond") on the ground in an open space indoors or outdoors. It will represent a pond.
- Place green circles ("lily pads") of butcher paper on the pond. Place the lily pads close enough so the children can jump safely from one to the next.
- Cut out numbers and place one on each lily pad.
  Note: Tape everything down for security.
- Decorate the rest of the pond with stuffed frogs, ducks, and so on.

WHAT TO DO
1. Gather the children around the pond. Ask the children what they think it is.
2. Call the children's attention to the numbers on the lily pads. Ask if they can name the numbers.
3. Tell the children that they are going to take turns being frogs. They are going to jump from lily pad to lily pad and count while jumping, starting with number one.
4. Call on a child to start. He can jump to hoop one and count or say, "One!" The other children can say and count as they jump too.
5. Be sure each child gets a chance to hop across the lily pads.

ASSESSMENT
To assess the children's learning, consider the following:
- Can the children count and say the numbers as they jump?
- When shown a number, can the children name what it is?

Shelley Hoster, Norcross, GA

Children's Books

Counting Crocodiles by
Judy Sierra
*In the Small, Small
Pond* by
Denise Fleming
Jump, Frog, Jump! by
Robert Kalan

Number Car Parade

3+

LEARNING OBJECTIVES

The children will:
1. Identify numbers.
2. Improve large motor skills.

Materials

10 large paper
 boxes
construction paper
 numbers 1–10
 or number cards
construction paper
 wheels

VOCABULARY

| car | numbers | wheels |
| move | push | |

PREPARATION

● Attach four paper wheels to each box so that they look like a car.
● Attach a large colored paper number or number card to the sides of each car.

WHAT TO DO

1. Display the numbered cars in a large open area of the classroom.
2. Invite the children to select a car and identify the number aloud.
3. Have the children push the car around the room, being careful not to bump into anything or anyone.
4. Have the children return the car to the starting point, select another car and repeat the activity as they practice identifying numbers.

TEACHER-TO-TEACHER TIP

● Use masking tape to create a car "track" for children to follow as they push their cars around the room.

ASSESSMENT

To assess the children's learning, consider the following:
● Display cars 1–5 in random order. Can the children move the cars so that they are in order from 1–5?
● Display the 10 cars in random order at the front of the room. Can the children move the cars so that they are in order from 1–10?
● Can each child identify numbers 1–10?

Mary J. Murray, Mazomanie, WI

Children's Books

All About Race Cars by
 Russ Flint
First Look at Cars by
 Daphne Butler
The Story of Cars by
 Howard W. Kanetzke

Popcorn Jump

3+

LEARNING OBJECTIVES

The children will:

1. Learn to follow a countdown from 10–1.
2. Develop listening skills and develop their awareness of sound and silence.

Materials

yoga mats
(optional)

VOCABULARY

loud   movement   quiet   stillness

WHAT TO DO

1. Have the children squat in a circle in an open area (or place yoga mats in a circle and squat on these).
2. Crouch down with the children and hold up your hand showing three fingers. Count down verbally as you take away one finger at a time: "Three! Two! One! Jump!"
3. Jump like popcorn up into the air, and land in the same spot in a crouching position.
4. Repeat and have the children countdown with you. You can build the anticipation by counting down from four, five, or any number up to 10.
5. Finally, have the children shout, "Popcorn!" as they jump in the air.

TEACHER-TO-TEACHER TIP

- After doing a verbal countdown several times, tell the children that your fingers are now going to do the count, in silence. "Watch closely!" How quiet can they be while waiting to jump and shout? After this you might choose to do the count and the jump in silence (though this is maybe not as fun).

ASSESSMENT

To assess the children's learning, consider the following:

- Do the children enjoy the anticipation of waiting for the big jump?
- When doing the silent countdown version, do the children become aware of the sounds in the room and the sounds that they are making?

Patrick Mitchell, Yagoto, Nagoya, Japan

Children's Books

The Popcorn Book by
Tomie dePaola
The Popcorn Dragon by
Jane Thayer and
Lisa McCue
Ten, Nine, Eight by
Molly Bang

The Counting Path

4+

LEARNING OBJECTIVES

The children will:
1. Identify the numbers in order.
2. Step on the circles with alternating feet maintaining balance.
3. Take turns and cooperate.

Materials

chalk or washable paint

VOCABULARY

circle	end	number names 1–10	order start

PREPARATION

● Use chalk or paint to make a long pathway of circles (about 10" in diameter and about 5" apart).

WHAT TO DO

1. Write "start" in the first circle and "end" in the last. Draw numbers inside all of the circles between, beginning with 1 and continuing in sequential order.
2. Ask the children to call out the number as they step on each circle.
3. On another day, try this activity again but mix up the numbers.

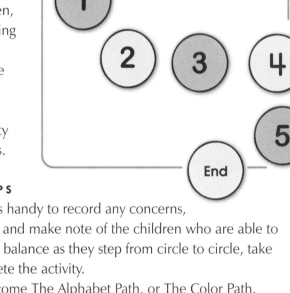

TEACHER-TO-TEACHER TIPS

● It is helpful to have notecards handy to record any concerns, issues, or highlights. Observe and make note of the children who are able to recite the numbers, maintain balance as they step from circle to circle, take turns, cooperate, and complete the activity.
● The Counting Path could become The Alphabet Path, or The Color Path.

Children's Books

12 Ways to Get to 11 by Eve Merriam
26 Letters and 99 Cents by Tana Hoban
One Hundred Hungry Ants by Elinor J. Pinczes

ASSESSMENT

To assess the children's learning, consider the following:
● Can the children count and recite the numbers?
● Can the children maintain their balance as they walk the path?

Judy Fujawa, The Villages, FL

Making Numbers with Bodies

4+

Materials

No materials necessary

LEARNING OBJECTIVES

The children will:

1. Learn the shapes of numbers through body movements.
2. Learn to cooperate with one another to create numbers with their bodies.

VOCABULARY

number   shape

WHAT TO DO

1. Ask the children to lie down on the floor, name a number, and create numbers with their bodies.
2. First ask children to make numbers by themselves. For example, one child can make the number one by lying on the ground with his arms at his sides. One child can make the number two by lying on the ground, curving his hands together above his head and bending his knees so that his legs form the base of the number.
3. Have the children work together to make one number. Two children together can form the number four. One child is the straight line and another child is the top portion of the number.
4. Two children together can form the number 0. Ask a group of children to form the number "40."
5. To extend the activity, take pictures of the children from above to show them their "body numbers." Or, make teams in the class and see who can form the number the fastest. Or, see if all of the children can make a number together.

ASSESSMENT

To assess the children's learning, consider the following:

- Can the children create numbers with their bodies?
- Can the children work cooperatively?
- Can the children recognize the shape of the numbers?

Michelle Barnea, Millburn, NJ

Children's Books

Mother Goose Numbers on the Loose by Leo and Diane Dillon
One to Ten by Chuck Murphy
Spot's Colors, Shapes, and Numbers by Eric Hill

Number Jump

4+

LEARNING OBJECTIVES

The children will:

1. Improve their large motor skills.
2. Recognize numbers.
3. Name numbers in unison.

step stool
number cards (6″
  or larger)
scissors (adult only)
hole punch
yarn

VOCABULARY

down	numbers	step	up
jump			

PREPARATION

● Punch two holes in each number card and string strands of yarn through the two holes to create number card necklaces.

WHAT TO DO

1. Display the step stool at the front of the class.
2. Invite half the children to line up behind the step stool.
3. Hand a number card necklace to each child in line.
4. Invite the children in the "audience" to be ready to announce numbers as their classmates step up onto the step stool.
5. Invite the first person in line to step up and display their number card necklace.
6. Listen to the children recite the number aloud in unison.
7. Instruct the child to jump off and return to the end of the line.
8. Repeat the activity several times until the children have jumped at least three times.
9. Exchange groups of children and repeat the activity again.

TEACHER-TO-TEACHER TIP

● Try this activity by asking children to slide down a slide outdoors in place of jumping from the step stool.

Children's Books

My Numbers by
  Neil Ricklen
Numbers and Sports by
  J. M. Patten
P.B. Bear's Numbers by
  Lee Davis

ASSESSMENT

To assess the children's learning, consider the following:

● Invite one or two children to wrap the yarn around each necklace as you put them away into a box. Can the children name each number as they help you?
● Give the children number-card necklaces in random order. Can each child put the necklaces back in the correct order?

Mary J. Murray, Mazomanie, WI

Paper Ball Kick

4+

LEARNING OBJECTIVES

The children will:
1. Identify numbers.
2. Improve their large motor skills.
3. Learn to be considerate of others when moving around the room.

Materials

several different colors of copy paper
whistle

VOCABULARY

crumble	kick	paper
foot	numbers	wrinkled

PREPARATION

● Write numbers 1–5 (or 10, or 20) in a random order on a sheet of paper. Create one sheet for each child using several different colors of paper.

WHAT TO DO

1. Provide each child with one sheet of paper.
2. Invite the children to crumble up their paper into a ball shape.
3. On the given command, the children find their own space in the room and begin kicking their paper ball around the room. Children are to follow their own ball wherever it lands and kick it again.
4. Blow a whistle to signal the children to stop kicking.
5. At that time, the children can pick up their paper balls, open them up and recite the numbers aloud.
6. Children can exchange papers with a classmate and the activity begins again.
7. Continue until the children have had the opportunity to kick several different colored paper balls and recite the numbers aloud.
8. To extend the activity, invite the children to line up in a row and throw the balls as far as possible. Then have the children run to their ball and throw it again in the same direction. Finally have the children open their paper and read the numbers aloud. Repeat the activity, throwing in the opposite direction.

ASSESSMENT

To assess the children's learning, consider the following:
● Can each child read his numbers aloud one at a time?
● Can each child point to each number as he recites it?

Mary J. Murray, Mazomanie, WI

Children's Books

Counting Colors by Roger Priddy
Kick the Ball, Marcie! by Charles M. Schulz
Numbers and Sports by J. M. Patten

Walk in the Rain

4+

LEARNING OBJECTIVES

The children will:

1. Improve their large motor skills.
2. Recognize numbers.
3. Role-play.

blue felt
scissors (adult only)
large number cards
rainy day sounds
   CD
child's umbrella

VOCABULARY

coat   step   umbrella   wet
rain

PREPARATION

- Cut 10 puddle shapes from blue felt. Display the puddles randomly about the game area.
- Display a large number card near each puddle.

WHAT TO DO

1. Turn on the rainy day sounds CD and ask the children to listen to the sounds of rain.
2. Invite one child to open up the umbrella.
3. Ask the selected child to step from puddle to puddle as the rest of the class watches and identifies the number near each puddle.
4. After the child has stepped in several puddles, he may hand the umbrella to another child.
5. Repeat the activity several times.
6. As an extension, make the materials available for the children to use independently during free time.

ASSESSMENT

To assess the children's learning, consider the following:

- Invite each child to hop from puddle to puddle. Can he identify the numbers?
- Place an assortment of number cards inside a folded umbrella. Invite a child to open the umbrella so the number cards spill out onto the floor. Can the child set the umbrella up on the floor and place the number cards in order from 1–5 or 1–10 beneath the umbrella?

Mary J. Murray, Mazomanie, WI

Children's Books

Rain by Alana
   Willoughby
Rain by Robert Kalan
The Rain by
Michael Laser

Counting Containers

3+

LEARNING OBJECTIVES

The children will:
1. Manipulate objects to count.
2. Count with one-to-one correspondence.
3. Begin to recognize numbers.

plastic apple
  containers from
  the grocery store
objects to count:
  pinecones or
  rocks or
  seashells

VOCABULARY

add   count   number   subtract

PREPARATION

- Save a plastic fruit container (the type apples are sold in) from the grocery store, or use the kind that have compartments for fruit.
- Write a number on each indent if you would like the children to match the number as they count. Write numbers on small labels with a permanent marker.
- Collect a number of items to count and place in a container.

WHAT TO DO

1. Put the objects and the counting container out for the children to explore.
2. Allow the children plenty of time to manipulate the objects and discover what they can do with the container, counting the objects as they place one at a time in each indentation.
3. When the children have had experience counting, you can wonder aloud how many there would be if you added one more, or subtracted one.
4. Later, ask the children to try counting backwards.

ASSESSMENT

To assess the children's learning, consider the following:

- When counting, do the children point to the object? Do the children touch the object? Do the children move an object as they count it?
- When the tray is empty, ask the children where a particular number is. Can the children find it? Do the children need to count in order to find the number or can they recognize it?

Laura Durbrow, Lake Oswego, OR

Children's Books

Arlene Alda's 1 2 3 by
Arlene Alda
Chicka Chicka 1 2 3 by
Bill Martin, Jr.
*My Very First Number
Book* by Angela Wilkes
Ten Little Ladybugs by
Melanie Gerth
*There Were Ten in the
Bed* by Pam Adams

Song

"Five Little Monkeys"

Dino Counting

4+

LEARNING OBJECTIVES
The children will:
1. Practice counting to 10.
2. Associate amounts with correlating numbers.
3. Compare large numbers to small.

Materials

card stock
scissors (adult only)
marker
55 small dinosaurs
   or other
   manipulatives

VOCABULARY
count   less than   more than   most
least

PREPARATION
- Cut the card stock into 3" x 5" pieces.
- Make number cards by writing one large number from 1–5 (or 10) at the top of each card. Also make the same number of dots as the number on each card.

WHAT TO DO
1. Set the number cards out in numerical order in a straight line.
2. Ask the children to touch each card and count at the same time.
3. While taking turns, have the children count the number of dinosaurs that belongs on each card, then place the dinosaurs on the card.

4. When every card is filled, ask the children, "Which card has the most dinosaurs?" "Which has the least?" "Does number eight have more than number two?" and so on.

TEACHER-TO-TEACHER TIP
- Be sure to provide some play time before and after the activity because the children may want to free play with the dinosaurs.

ASSESSMENT
To assess the children's learning, consider the following:
- Can the children compare the amounts on the cards?
- Can the children use terminology related to amounts (like "most")?
- Can the children count to five (or 10)?

Children's Books

*How Do Dinosaurs
Count to Ten?* by
Jane Yolen
Ten Little Dinosaurs by
Pattie Schnetzler and
Jim Harris
Ten Terrible Dinosaurs
by Paul Stickland

Jaclyn Miller, Mishawaka, IN

Number Touch

4+

LEARNING OBJECTIVES

The children will:

1. Recognize the shape of numbers 1–10.
2. Recognize the number names 1–10.
3. Count in sequence from 1–10.
4. Practice small motor skills.

Materials

textured wallpaper
  or carpet scraps
10 pieces of
  cardboard at
  least 7″ high and
  6″ wide
glue
scissors (adult only)
ruler
10 3″ x 5″ cards
thick permanent
  marker in dark
  color

VOCABULARY

count   match   shape   texture

PREPARATION

- From the textured material, cut numbers 1–10 at least 5″ tall and 1″ wide.
- Glue each number onto a cardboard piece. Let dry.
- On 3″ x 5″ cards, print one number from 1–10.

WHAT TO DO

1. This may take several days, depending on the age and ability of the children. You may want to start with only three numbers and work up to 10. Let the children trace the textured numbers with their fingers, as if writing.
2. As you say the name of each number, invite each child to trace the number and repeat its name.
3. Show a 3″ x 5″ card and have the children tell you which number matches the textured number.
4. Count in sequence from 1–10, pointing to each number. Invite the children to count along with you. Display textured numbers where the children can touch them whenever they choose.

ASSESSMENT

To assess the children's learning, consider the following:

- Can the children trace numbers?
- Can the children identify the names of numbers?

Kay Flowers, Summerfield, OH

Children's Books

How Do Dinosaurs Count to Ten? by Jane Yolen
Pat the Bunny by Dorothy Kunhardt
Ten Black Dots by Donald Crews

Poem and Song

"One, Two, Buckle My Shoe"
"This Old Man"

Number Yolk Fun

4+

LEARNING OBJECTIVES
The children will:
1. Recognize and name written numbers 1–10.
2. Match pairs of numbers 1–10.

plastic eggs that
    open and close
scissors (adult only)
number yolk
    cutouts
large poster board
    for egg game
    board

VOCABULARY
chicken   frying pan   spatula   yolk
egg

PREPARATION
- Prepare number "yolks" by cutting out yellow circles and numbering each yolk from 1–10. Laminate for durability.
- Write corresponding numbers on poster board.

WHAT TO DO
1. Place one number circle in each plastic egg.
2. The children can simulate "cracking" their egg and matching their number in the egg to the same number on the game board.
3. If the children can count past 10, make it a little more challenging by making egg numbers and corresponding numbers on the board up to 20.
4. For extra fun with this game in the math center, store your eggs in a frying pan with a real spatula. Great in the dramatic play area as well!

ASSESSMENT
To assess the children's learning, consider the following:
- Can the children recognize and name written numbers from 1–10?
- Can the children match pairs of numbers 1–10?

Jason Verdone, Woodbury, NJ

Children's Books

Big Fat Hen by
Keith Baker
*My Very First Book of
Numbers* by Eric Carle
Numbers by
Melanie Watt

Soup Pot Numbers

LEARNING OBJECTIVES

The children will:
1. Count numbers.
2. Create their own soup pot of numbers.

Materials

poster with
   numbers from
   1–10
copy paper
marker
paper numbers
crayons
felt

VOCABULARY

numbers	pot	three
one	soup	two

PREPARATION

● Place a poster of numbers 1–10 on the wall in the classroom.
● Draw an empty soup pot on a white piece of paper. Photocopy enough for each child.
● Cut out a felt soup pot and felt numbers 1–10.

WHAT TO DO

1. Point to each number on the poster. Ask the children to identify each number. Count with them.
2. Pass out a paper with an empty soup pot. Give the children their own set of paper numbers. Ask them to glue the numbers in the soup. Give them crayons to add color to their soup.
3. Put all but one of the numbers on the felt soup pot. Say, "Look at the felt soup pot. One number from 1–10 is missing. Which one is not there?" Help the children identify the missing number by counting the numbers.
4. Ask the children to write their names on the papers and practice writing numbers.

TEACHER-TO-TEACHER TIP

● Ask the children to say the numbers as they glue them on their papers. Use other props like posters to reinforce the numbers visually.

ASSESSMENT

To assess the children's learning, consider the following:
● Put the children's soup pot numbers on the wall. Can the children tell you about their soup pots?
● When you take one of the numbers out of the soup pot, can the children tell you which number is missing?
● Can the children count the numbers in the soup pot?

Children's Books

Fun with Counting by
Jenny Ackland
Numbers 1–10 by
Lois Bottoni
Stone Soup by
Marcia Brown

Lily Erlic, Victoria, British Columbia, Canada

Supermarket

LEARNING OBJECTIVES

The children will:

1. Manipulate money.
2. Learn that different objects have different values.
3. Learn that they can find similar items that are less expensive at another store.

Materials

play money (or colored strips of paper)

things to buy or do (stickers, gum, small toys, pencils, erasers, snacks, play a game, blow bubbles)

"supermarket" centers (decorated tables)

cashiers (aides, family members, or children)

poster board

shopping bags

VOCABULARY

allowance   coupon   expensive   quality

budget

PREPARATION

● Create 5–10 "supermarket" centers. Place available items in each center, along with a price list hung on the wall beside each one (written on poster board).

WHAT TO DO

1. Explain to the children that they will be going shopping. Point out the supermarkets and businesses around the room.
2. Show the children the play money. Count the money with the children.
3. Demonstrate how to purchase these items and activities (for example, one red = a stick of gum, two blues = a minute to blow bubbles).
4. Hand out the money and shopping bags to the children. Invite them to use their money in any way they choose.
5. Suggest to the children that they walk around first, exploring all of their options. Explain that there may be identical items in two different stores, one of which may be less expensive.

ASSESSMENT

To assess the children's learning, consider the following:

● Do the children understand the concept of many?
● Was it hard for the children to look around first before buying something?

Angela Hawkins, Denver, CO

Children's Books

Bunny Money by Rosemary Wells

How Much Is a Million? by David M. Schwartz

One, Two, Buckle My Shoe: A Book of Counting Rhymes by Rowan Barnes-Murphy

The Story of Money by Betsy Maestro and Giulio Maestro

Cars on Roads

3+

LEARNING OBJECTIVES

The children will:
1. Improve number writing skills.
2. Improve motor skills.
3. Improve oral language skills.
4. Follow directions.

Materials

10 toy cars or
trucks
black paper

VOCABULARY

car	fast	slow
drive	road	truck

PREPARATION

- Cut large numbers from 1–10 from the black paper.
- Use chalk to draw a dotted line down the center of each number so that it looks like a road.
- Draw a green circle at the beginning of each number and a red circle at the end of each number.

WHAT TO DO

1. Invite the children to manipulate a car as they learn more about writing numbers.
2. Have the children place their car at the "green light" starting point on each number.
3. Invite the children to drive their car along the road until they come to the "red light." Once the children stop at the end of the number, have them take their car and move on to a different number.
4. Encourage the children to drive a car along all 10 numbers.

ASSESSMENT

To assess the children's learning, consider the following:
- Can each child identify the numbers and stop and go as directed by the red and green lights?
- Draw a grid of 10 spaces on a sheet of construction paper. Write a number in each space and each of the corresponding numbers on one car. Can the children drive their cars into the "garage" with the matching number?

Mary J. Murray, Mazomanie, WI

Children's Books

Bears on Wheels by
Stan Berenstain and
Jan Berenstain
Count! by
Denise Fleming
Numbers and Speed by
J. M. Patten

Number Wall

3+

LEARNING OBJECTIVES

The children will:
1. Use their sense of touch and sight.
2. Identify numbers.
3. Improve their vocabulary and oral language skills.

materials with a
   variety of
   textures:
   sandpaper,
   corrugated
   cardboard,
   bubble wrap,
   aluminum foil,
   imitation fur
   fabric, imitation
   suede fabric,
   and fleece
scissors (adult only)
glue
brightly colored tag
   board or
   construction
   paper

VOCABULARY

bumpy	hands	smooth
feel	rough	touch

PREPARATION

- Cut a large number from each type of textured material.
- Glue each number to a colorful sheet of paper or tag board and let dry.
- Hang the large number cards in random order, at the children's level, along the length of a wall in the classroom.

WHAT TO DO

1. Invite the children to line up at one end of the "Number Wall."
2. Encourage the children to travel slowly down the length of the wall, using their sense of touch to feel each number.
3. Have the children identify each number and describe how it feels.
4. Once the children have touched every number, invite them to go to the end of the line to repeat the activity.
5. Afterward, encourage the children to talk about the experience as they identify the various materials from which the numbers were cut.

TEACHER-TO-TEACHER TIPS

- Use this sensory activity as a means of organizing children to transition from one activity in the classroom to another.
- Make a small version of this activity and place this set of touchable number cards in a basket. Invite small groups of children to work with the materials as you observe them identifying numbers.

ASSESSMENT

To assess the children's learning, consider the following:
- Take turns covering the eyes of each child. As he touches a number, can he identify the number?
- Can each child recognize, describe, and name each number on the "Number Wall?"

Children's Books

Anno's Counting House
   by Mitsumasa Anno
Touch by Maria Rius
The Very Busy Spider by
   Eric Carle

Mary J. Murray, Mazomanie, WI

Sock Sort

3+

LEARNING OBJECTIVES

The children will:

1. Match like socks together.
2. Match like numbers together.
3. Identify numbers.
4. Order numbers.

Materials

10 or more pairs of
   socks
colored duct tape
   or electrical tape
bold permanent
   marker
laundry basket
clothesline and
   clothespins
   (optional)

VOCABULARY

color	number	sock
match	pair	two

PREPARATION

- Use the marker to print numbers 1–10 on the colored tape. Make two of each number.
- Cut the numbers apart.
- Lay the pairs of socks flat on the table and attach each pair of numbers to a pair of socks.
- Place the socks in the laundry basket.
- Display the clothesline and clothespins with the socks, if applicable.

WHAT TO DO

1. Invite a small group of children to spill out the basket of socks.
2. Challenge the children to match the socks by their numbers and place them together in pairs on the floor.
3. Ask the children to name the numbers on the socks and identify their color.
4. Have the children place the pairs of socks in order from 1–10.
5. If applicable, invite the children to hang the pairs of socks, in order, along the clothesline.

TEACHER-TO-TEACHER TIP

- If you do not have an assortment of socks, simply cut pairs of paper socks from colored construction paper and write a number on each.

ASSESSMENT

To assess the children's learning, consider the following:

- Give the children one of the numbered pairs of socks and hang the second sock on a clothesline. Can the children match their socks to the correct hanging socks?
- Can the children roll the socks into balls, toss them to one another, unroll them, and identify the numbers on each sock?

Children's Books

Clothes by
Fiona Pragoff
*Is It Larger? Is It
Smaller?* by
Tana Hoban
*One, Two, Buckle My
Shoe: A Book of
Counting Rhymes* by
Rowan Barnes-Murphy
A Pair of Socks by
Stuart J. Murphy

Mary J. Murray, Mazomanie, WI

How Many Hatching Chicks?

4+

Materials

3–5 plastic eggs
20 medium-sized yellow pompoms

LEARNING OBJECTIVES

The children will:
1. Learn that numbers can be grouped in order to aid in counting (this will lay foundations for multiplication).
2. Learn to follow specific directions.

VOCABULARY

chick   hatch   number names

WHAT TO DO

1. Begin the activity by showing the children one yellow pompom.
2. Explain that this will represent a newly hatched chick. Place the pompom into an egg, close the egg, and open it again. Show the children that one chick hatched from the egg.
3. Next, place two pompoms in one egg and repeat the actions. Ask the children to count the chicks that hatch from the egg.
4. Next, place two pompoms in two eggs (total of four). Ask the children to guess how many chicks are going to hatch. "Hatch" the eggs and let the children count the number of chicks that hatch.
5. Continue the activity with different numbers of eggs and chicks. If children are catching on, try having them count before the eggs hatch. For example, put two chicks in three eggs. Make sure the children understand that each egg has two chicks in it.
6. Ask the children to count the chicks without opening the eggs. Hold up each egg and count "One, two, and three, four...and five, six!"

TEACHER-TO-TEACHER TIP

- By changing the number of chicks in each egg, you can introduce both addition and multiplication basics. Let the children take turns creating combinations to count.

ASSESSMENT

To assess the children's learning, consider the following:
- Are the children able to follow directions?
- To what extent do the children grasp the concept of grouping numbers?

Children's Books

12 Ways to Get to 11 by Eve Merriam
The Crayon Counting Book by Pam Munoz and Jerry Pallotta
Fun with Counting by Jenny Ackland

Sarah Stasik, Bent Mountain, VA

Let's Count How Many

4+

LEARNING OBJECTIVES

The children will:
1. Participate in the counting experience.
2. Start counting and playing with math ideas on their own.
3. Show signs of wanting to do more advanced counting games and paperwork.

Materials

record-keeping
chart

VOCABULARY

count	less	object	set
more			

PREPARATION

- Read books, sing songs, and repeat fingerplays about counting.
- Talk with the children about counting one-to-one, identifying more and less, distinguishing higher and lower numbers, and so on.

WHAT TO DO

1. On a regular basis, ask the children to "count how many" objects there are in the room. Begin with easy and simple counting, such as three windows, eight tables, or 10 trucks. Then, start counting items that require more advanced counting skills, such as 20 markers, 45 beads, 60 pegs, or 104 blocks. Each time you count items, record that number on a record-keeping chart for easy reference.
2. Extend this counting activity by counting the number of days in one month and then continuing on for the entire school term.

TEACHER-TO-TEACHER TIP

- Make the children aware of identifying numbers and counting. Environmental print is a good way for them to make these observations. Ask questions that require the children to recall "how many," "which had more," and so on. Invite the children to share and show their own ideas to the other children in the class.

Children's Books

Count and See by
Tana Hoban
Counting Colors by
Roger Priddy
How Much Is a Million?
by David M. Schwartz

ASSESSMENT

To assess the children's learning, consider the following:
- Make both mental and written notes of any concerns, issues, or highlights. Are any of the children ready to move on to more advanced math experiences?
- Do the children feel comfortable sharing and showing their own ideas to the other children in the class?

Judy Fujawa, The Villages, FL

My Favorite Toys

4+

LEARNING OBJECTIVES

The children will:
1. Learn the names of ordinal numbers.
2. Learn the sequence of ordinal numbers.
3. Learn to relate ordinal numbers to concrete objects.

Materials

wide selection of animals or small toys
sets of cards with ordinal numbers

VOCABULARY

favorite	first	second
fifth	fourth	third

PREPARATION

● Make cards of the first five ordinal numbers (1st, 2nd, and so on).

WHAT TO DO

1. Explain ordinal numbers to the children and show them the cards representing the numbers.
2. Tell the children to choose their five favorite toys in the room.
3. Then give each child a set of ordinal cards and ask him to choose which toy he likes best and put the "1st" card in front of it.
4. Ask the children to put all five toys in order and label them with the ordinal cards.
5. Encourage the children to take turns to vocalize their ordinal list: "My favorite toys are: first, a red fire truck; second, a kangaroo; third, a car jigsaw puzzle; fourth, stickle bricks; and fifth, a racing car."

TEACHER-TO-TEACHER TIP

● It is best to do this favorite toy activity with only a few children at a time to prevent arguments when children have similar favorites.

ASSESSMENT

To assess the children's learning, consider the following:
● Can the children recite the ordinal numbers correctly?
● Can the children put ordinal numbers into the correct sequence?
● Can the children relate ordinal numbers to concrete objects, such as toys?

Anne Adeney, Plymouth, England, United Kingdom

Children's Books

First, Second by Daniil Kharms
My Most Favorite Thing by Nicola Moon
Snow? Let's Go! by Karen Berman Nagel

Number Touch

4+

LEARNING OBJECTIVES

The children will:

1. Learn to identify numbers.
2. Learn to recognize numbers by their shapes.

Materials

thick plastic
   numbers 1–9
large tray
dark cloth large
   enough to cover
   the tray

VOCABULARY

curved   number   straight

WHAT TO DO

1. Show the children the plastic numbers 1, 2, and 3. Discuss the straight lines of the 1, the curving and straight lines of the 2, and the curved lines of the 3.
2. Let the children have a turn to feel the numbers. Encourage them to discuss the way the numbers feel.
3. Put them on the tray and cover them with the dark cloth. Reach under the cloth and move the numbers around.
4. Ask a child to touch one of the numbers through the cloth, feel it, identify it, and then reach under the cloth and bring out the number to show the other children.
5. After the child puts the number back, ask another child to touch a number.
6. When these numbers are easily identified by the children, add 4 and 5.
7. Continue adding the rest of the numbers as the children grow skilled in identifying the first set.

TEACHER-TO-TEACHER TIP

- Encourage the children to make curved and straight lines with their arms when you talk about the curved and straight lines of the numbers.

ASSESSMENT

To assess the children's learning, consider the following:
- Can each child identify the plastic numbers?
- Can each child recognize the numbers by their shapes?

Susan Oldham Hill, Lakeland, FL

Children's Books

Knots on a Counting Rope by Bill Martin, Jr.
Moja Means One by Muriel Feelings
One Gorilla: A Counting Book by Atsuko Morozumi

One Dozen Equals 12

4+

LEARNING OBJECTIVES

The children will:

1. Interact cooperatively with other children.
2. Begin to understand the concept of one dozen.

Materials

egg cartons
muffin tins
cookie sheets
playdough
tools to use with
  playdough:
  plastic knives,
  rolling pins,
  measuring
  spoons and
  cookie cutters
small objects, such
  as beads,
  buttons, small
  cars, and so on

VOCABULARY

dozen   half dozen   six-pack   twelve

PREPARATION

- Discuss the concept of one dozen with the children.
- Show the children a dozen eggs, a dozen donuts, a cupcake baking tray with 12 cupcake holders, and so on.

WHAT TO DO

1. Count out 12 items for each egg carton and muffin tin.
2. Ask the children to fill the egg cartons and tins with a dozen (12) items.
3. Allow the children to search the room for a dozen items to place in the carton or tins, such as beads, buttons, small cars, and so on.
4. Ask the children to make a dozen "cookies" using playdough.

TEACHER-TO-TEACHER TIP

- It is important to incorporate everyday items and environmental print into the conversation. For example, "a dozen eggs," "a dozen donuts," "a dozen cupcakes," and so on. Many items are packaged in "half dozen" or six-packs, such as yogurt, soft drinks, and bottled water. Invite the children to share and show their own ideas with the rest of the class.

ASSESSMENT

To assess the children's learning, consider the following:

- Are the children interested in counting or just happy to mold and pound the playdough?
- Are the children taking part in conversation?
- Are the children ready, willing, and able to cooperate and share the items on the table?
- Are the children showing signs of moving on to more advanced counting?

Judy Fujawa, The Villages, FL

Children's Books

Big Fat Hen by Keith Baker
Fun with Counting by Jenny Ackland
Roll Over! A Counting Song by Merle Peek

Stand-Out Numbers

4+

The children will:

1. Recognize numbers.
2. Learn to cooperate with one another.

Materials

foam sheets
scissors (adult only)
double-sided tape
copy paper
crayons
set of number
cards

VOCABULARY

foam   rubbing

PREPARATION

- Cut 4" numbers from foam sheets and stick them to a table with double-sided tape.
- Group three foam numbers close enough so they will fit on a piece of copy paper.
- Remove the paper wrappers from old crayon pieces.

WHAT TO DO

1. Show the children how to work with a partner: one child holds the paper still while another child makes a crayon rubbing.
2. Ask a child to hold a piece of copy paper over a set of three numbers taped to the table.
3. While the first child keeps the paper still, show the second child how to rub over the foam shapes with the side of the unwrapped crayon to make the number appear.
4. Remind the children to make sure their partners hold the papers still or the numbers will look too fuzzy to recognize.

ASSESSMENT

To assess the children's learning, consider the following:

- If you show the children the set of number cards in random order, can they name the numbers?
- Do the children cooperate with one another to complete the task?

Susan Oldham Hill, Lakeland, FL

Children's Books

1 Is One by
Tasha Tudor
12 Ways to Get to 11
by Eve Merriam
*One Child, One Seed:
A South African
Counting Book* by
Kathryn Cave

Weighing In

4+

LEARNING OBJECTIVES

The children will:
1. Discover their weight.
2. Observe a class graph.

poster board
white copy paper
crayons
felt pens
scale

VOCABULARY

graph	more than	scale	weight
less than	pounds	weigh	

PREPARATION

● Place a large piece of plain poster board on the wall and draw a graph. Write the names of each child along the bottom of the graph. Down the side, write numbers from 10–60.
● Draw a scale on a sheet of copy paper and copy enough for each child.

WHAT TO DO

1. Use the scale to weigh each child in the class. Write down their weights on a piece of paper.
2. With the children, make a bar graph so the children can see the different weights in the classroom. Explain what the graph shows.
3. Say, "This is how much everyone weighs. How many children weigh more than 40 pounds? How many children weigh less than 40 pounds?" Compare weights. "How much does the whole class weigh?"
4. Give each child a scale sheet, crayons, and felt. Ask the child to color his paper scale. Help each child print his weight at the top and his name at the bottom of the paper.

TEACHER-TO-TEACHER TIP

● Ask the children to say their weights as they print them in their books.

ASSESSMENT

To assess the children's learning, consider the following:
● What can the children tell you about their scales?
● Can each child tell you how much he weighs?
● Can the children tell you how much the class weighs together?

Lily Erlic, Victoria, British Columbia, Canada

Children's Books

How Heavy Is It? by Brian Sargent
Size by Henry Arthur Pluckrose
Weight by Henry Arthur Pluckrose

100 Day Bank

5+

LEARNING OBJECTIVES

The children will:

1. Count 100 pennies.
2. Exchange pennies for an uncirculated dollar bill.
3. Celebrate the 100th day of school by "visiting the bank."

Materials

Note to parents "100 Day Bank" made from a puppet theater or table

Uncirculated dollar bills and bank envelopes (one of each for each child)

A plastic jar "counter"

VOCABULARY

circulated   exchange   transaction   uncirculated

PREPARATION

- Send a note home asking parents to help their child save 100 pennies to bring in on "100 Day."
- Arrange to get uncirculated dollar bills and envelopes from your bank.
- Set up the bank in a quiet area.

WHAT TO DO

1. Ask the children to count their pennies, then stack them by fives and then by 10s.
2. Ask a child to volunteer to be the "banker." Your banker needs a large plastic container to hold the pennies and dollar bills and envelopes for exchange. Write the child's name on the envelope.
3. Have the children take turns visiting the bank to exchange pennies for dollar bills.
4. Engage the children in a discussion about the value of the 100 pennies and the dollar bill. Talk to them about the similarities and differences of the two forms of currency.

TEACHER-TO-TEACHER TIP

- Stress the importance of the child counting the pennies at home and putting the pennies in stacks to count by fives and 10s.

Children's Books

100th Day Worries by Margery Cuyler
Fun with Counting by Jenny Ackland
Miss Bindergarten Celebrates the 100th Day of Kindergarten by Joseph Slate

ASSESSMENT

To assess the children's learning, consider the following:

- Can the children count to 100?
- Can the children sort the pennies by stacks of five and 10?

Carol Zook, Fort Wayne, IN

Abacus Art

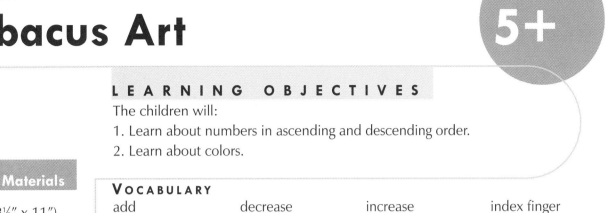

5+

LEARNING OBJECTIVES

The children will:
1. Learn about numbers in ascending and descending order.
2. Learn about colors.

Materials

paper (8½″ x 11″)
newspaper
crayons
pencil
fingerpaints
scale

VOCABULARY

add   decrease   increase   index finger

PREPARATION

● Create ruled paper (1″ width), 10 lines per sheet, with a margin. Turn the page so that the lines run horizontally like an abacus. Make a copy of this paper for each child in the classroom.
● Spread newspaper on the floor.

WHAT TO DO

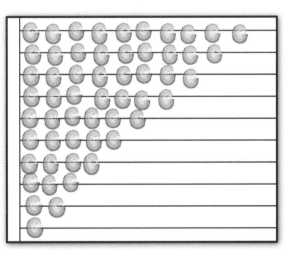

1. Divide the children into groups. Give each group one bowl of paint (a different color for each group). Distribute one paper to each child. Ask the children to dip their index finger in the paint and make 10 circles on the first line, nine circles on the second line, and so on.
2. Later, ask the children to count the total number of circles on each line and help them write the numbers under each line.
3. Consider including a model for children who need one. If necessary, start with five circles on a line instead of 10.

ASSESSMENT

To assess the children's learning, consider the following:
● Can the children count the number of lines on the page?
● Can the children identify the colors used in the exercise?

Shyamala Shanmugasundaram, Nerul, Navi Mumbai, India

Children's Books

Counting Colors by Roger Priddy
The Crayon Counting Book by Pam Munoz Ryan and Jerry Pallotta
Learning Block Books: Numbers, Colors, Shapes, Animals by Susan Estelle Kwas

Graphing Ice Cream Flavors

5+

Materials

sidewalk chalk
graph paper or
   tablecloth
   (optional)
4" x 4" paper
crayons
beanbags
ice cream

LEARNING OBJECTIVES

The children will:
1. Demonstrate an understanding of counting.
2. Think ahead and make simple predictions.
3. Translate totals into a graph.

VOCABULARY

counting	predict	sorting	total
graph			

PREPARATION

- Use sidewalk chalk to create a graph on playground blacktop. (Use large graph paper or a large white plastic tablecloth if you are unable to write on blacktop.)

WHAT TO DO

1. Ask each child what his favorite flavor of ice cream is. For their answers, have each children draw or color a picture of the ice cream cone of his choice on a 4" x 4" piece of paper.
2. Before sorting and counting the different flavors, ask the class to predict how many children might have chosen chocolate, vanilla, and strawberry ice cream cones.
3. As a class, sort and count each flavor and explain how to find a total for each flavor. Demonstrate on the blackboard or a large sheet of paper how to use a graph.
4. Take the children outside and have them place beanbags in sections of the graph to represent amounts.
5. Do this many times, so that all the children have a chance to participate. Then serve an ice cream treat to the children.

TEACHER-TO-TEACHER TIP

- On another day, sort different items that also interest the children.

ASSESSMENT

To assess the children's learning, consider the following:
- Can the child make predictions?
- Does the child understand how to use a graph to translate totals?

Children's Books

Adding It Up by
Rosemary Wells
*Exploring the Numbers
1–100* by
Mary Beth Spann
Sort, Graph, and Tally
by Amy Decastro

MaryLouise Alu Curto, Mercerville, NJ

Hungry Dog

5+

LEARNING OBJECTIVES

The children will:

1. Count objects from one to six.
2. Explore one-to-one correspondence with objects.

Materials

dog biscuits
dice
timer

VOCABULARY

biscuits	dog	number names	roll
die	hungry	from 1–6	

WHAT TO DO

1. Group the children in pairs. Give each child the same number of dog biscuits (start with 10–12). Give each pair a die. Set a timer for several minutes.
2. The children take turns rolling the die. One child rolls the die and counts the number of dots showing on the top of the die. He then counts out that number of dog biscuits from his pile and gives them to his hungry dog friend.
3. Then the partner takes a turn, following the same procedure.
4. When the timer goes off, the children count the bones they have in their piles. The hungry dog will have most or all of bones in his pile.
5. Start over with new partners.

ASSESSMENT

To assess the children's learning, consider the following:

● When a die is rolled, can the children match the same number of items shown on the die?
● When told a number between one and six, can the children count out the correct number of objects?

Monica Hay Cook, Tucson, AZ

Children's Books

Counting Colors by Roger Priddy
Ten Black Dots by Donald Crews
What a Hungry Puppy! by Gail Herman

Sad Mr. Zero

5+

LEARNING OBJECTIVES

The children will:

1. Learn that the number zero adds nothing.
2. Learn small equations.

Materials

poster board
marker
scissors (adult only)

VOCABULARY

addition   plus   subtraction   zero

PREPARATION

- Cut the poster board into cards.
- Create pairs of numbers from 1–10 from poster board. Laminate them for durability if desired.
- For each number, draw and cut out a smiley face with the number as the nose, except for the number 0. Also cut out a plus sign and an equal sign. Make a frown face with the number zero as the nose.

WHAT TO DO

1. Give each child a number or a function card to hold; for example, a 2 or a plus sign.
2. Explain that numbers are like a party—the more there are, the more fun they have. The only one who doesn't add any fun is Sad Mr. Zero because "he has nothing to add."
3. This lesson should help the children learn that zero adds nothing to a number. Ask different children to come up with their signs and make an equation using one number and adding zero.
4. Each time, everyone can be sad and pretend to cry when Sad Mr. Zero comes up because he has "nothing to add."

TEACHER-TO-TEACHER TIP

- The more the children cry and carry on, the more they learn that Sad Mr. Zero has nothing to add!

Children's Books

The Crayon Counting Book by Pam Munoz Ryand and Jerry Pallotta
Numbers by Melanie Watt
Safari Animals by Paul Hess

ASSESSMENT

To assess the children's learning, consider the following:

- Does each child understand the concept of zero?
- Can the children understand beginning equations?

Susan Lancaster, Knoxville, TN

Time It

5+

LEARNING OBJECTIVES

The children will:
1. Repeat numbers 1–10 (and higher).
2. Learn to count to 10 (and higher).

Materials

small hourglass or kitchen timer
chart paper and marker

VOCABULARY

count　　　　　　number　　　　　　number names

WHAT TO DO

1. Pick a short activity that you can time. For example, tell the children you are going to see how long it takes to pass out napkins at snack time.
2. Count out loud. The children count along: one second, two seconds, three seconds, four seconds, five seconds, and so on.
3. Stop counting when the children have passed out all the napkins.
4. Each day choose a different child to pass out napkins.
5. Make a chart and record the time it takes to complete the task each day.
6. Select a different activity to time. Choose an activity that takes longer to complete.

TEACHER-TO-TEACHER TIP

● To vary the activity, try hourglass timers and kitchen timers. You can even see if an activity can be completed within a period of time.

ASSESSMENT

To assess the children's learning, consider the following:
● Can the children repeat numbers after you model saying them?
● Can the children to count from 1–10?

Monica Hay Cook, Tucson, AZ

Children's Books

Ten Little Dinosaurs by Pattie Schnetzler
Ten Little Fish by Audrey Wood
Ten Little Ladybugs by Melanie Gerth
Ten Little Mice by Joyce Dunbar
Ten Little Monkeys Jumping on the Bed by Tina Freeman
Ten Little Rabbits by Virginia Grossman

Good Morning, Numbers

3+

LEARNING OBJECTIVES

The children will:
1. Improve their number recognition skills.
2. Enhance their oral language skills.

Materials

paper sun
large card stock
  numbers, 1–10

VOCABULARY

good morning	Mrs.	number names	sun
Mr.		1–10	

PREPARATION

- Draw a simple face on each number.
- Add a mustache and top hat to designate a male number and eyelashes, blush, and flower in the hair to signify a female number.

WHAT TO DO

1. Display the numbers in front of the children.
2. Hold the paper sun above the first number on the left of the number line.
3. Invite the children to say, "Good morning, Mr. One!" (and continue with Mrs. Two, Mr. Three, and so on).
4. Reply to the children by saying "Good morning, children."
5. Move the sun from number to number as the children say good morning to each number.

TEACHER-TO-TEACHER TIPS

- Arrange the numbers in a different order each day of the week.
- Draw a large sun (20' diameter or larger) using yellow chalk on the playground. Write several numbers inside the sun. Invite the children to run around the sun. When you blow the whistle and say "Good Morning," the children step inside the sun and stand on a number. Invite the children to identify their number then return to running around the sun. Play several times until the children have identified a variety of numbers.

ASSESSMENT

To assess the children's learning, consider the following:
- Invite each child to come forward and say good morning to each number character one at a time. Can each child identify all 10 numbers?
- Create 10 paper suns. Print a number from 1–10 on each sun. Can the children match the paper suns to the paper numbers by matching like numbers?

Children's Books

Hello Sun by Hans Wilhelm
My Very First Book of Numbers by Eric Carle
Sunshine by Gail Saunders-Smith

Mary J. Murray, Mazomanie, WI

Jump and Shout

4+

LEARNING OBJECTIVES

The children will:

1. Improve their large motor skills.
2. Improve their number recognition skills.
3. Cooperate and take turns.

Materials

sidewalk chalk

VOCABULARY

hop	number names	shout	square
jump	1–10		

PREPARATION

- Use sidewalk chalk to create a 4' x 5', 20-square grid on the playground.
- Print a number between 1 and 10 (or 20) within each square.

WHAT TO DO

1. Have the children sit in rows on one side of the grid so the numbers are facing the children.
2. Invite two children to step onto the grid.
3. Encourage the children to jump to the other side of the grid from square to square and shout the name of each number as they land in the squares. Children may jump sideways or forward as they move across the grid.
4. Once a child reaches the other side, he calls the name of a classmate to go next and then returns to the end of the line.
5. Allow time for the children to have several opportunities to jump and shout numbers as they cross the grid.

TEACHER-TO-TEACHER TIP

- Use an old window shade or shower curtain and permanent marker to create an indoor version of this game.

Children's Books

123 Moose: A Pacific Northwest Counting Book by Andrea Halman
Feast for Ten by Cathryn Falwell
Numbers by David Stienecker

ASSESSMENT

To assess the children's learning, consider the following:

- As the children jump onto numbers and cross the grid, are they able to identify numbers 1–10 (or 20)?
- Can the children write numbers on the playground using chalk?
- Display a variety of large number cards randomly around the playground. Call out a number. Can the children run to sit near the select number?

Mary J. Murray, Mazomanie, WI

Let It Snow!

4+

LEARNING OBJECTIVES

The children will:
1. Practice writing numbers and shapes in snow.
2. Actively participate in an outdoor activity.

Materials

empty detergent containers (one per child)
food coloring in assorted colors

VOCABULARY

blizzard	snow drift	snowfall
snow ball	snow people	squeeze

PREPARATION

- Send a letter to family members in advance, describing your outdoor activity and asking them to send their child to school in warm clothing and boots, if possible.
- Have extra mittens and boots for children who arrive without them.
- Fill each detergent container with water.
- Add enough food coloring to make the water as dark as possible.

WHAT TO DO

1. In circle or group time announce that everyone will go outdoors for a special snow activity.
2. Help the children remember different numbers.
3. Call out numbers and ask the children to write them in the air with their hands.
4. Help the children dress for the outdoors.
5. Review outdoor behavior, snow safety, and school rules.
6. Once you are outdoors, distribute the containers and demonstrate how to squeeze the colored water out into the snow.
7. Allow the children to practice manipulating the container and water to make numbers in the snow.
8. Call out numbers for the children to write in the snow with their containers. Observe what they are doing. Return to the classroom and get warm!

TEACHER-TO-TEACHER TIP

- Extend the activity to shapes and colors.

ASSESSMENT

To assess the children's learning, consider the following:
- Were the children able to follow directions and manipulate the containers?
- Did the children draw the numbers somewhat accurately in the snow?

Children's Books

The Jacket I Wear in the Snow by Shirley Neitzel
Owl Moon by Jane Yolen
Snow Crazy by Tracy Gallup
Snowballs by Lois Ehlert
The Snowy Day by Ezra Jack Keats

Margery Kranyik Fermino, West Roxbury, MA

No-Fail Hopscotch

4+

LEARNING OBJECTIVES

The children will:

1. Practice number recognition for numbers 1–8.
2. Learn how to follow directions.
3. Practice large motor skills by hopping and jumping while maintaining balance.

Materials

hopscotch grid (in chalk on your blacktop, with tape on the floor, or on a hopscotch carpet)
chalk
small beanbags
balls

VOCABULARY

count   hop   jump   toss

PREPARATION

- Prepare a hopscotch grid with numbers 1–8.

WHAT TO DO

1. Assemble the children around your hopscotch grid.
2. Discuss or review how to hop and jump. For the purposes of this activity, encourage the children to "hop" on one foot and "jump" with both feet.
3. Demonstrate rules of traditional hopscotch and tell the children that they are going to do something special on the grid.
4. Invite each child to practice hopping or jumping into the square.
5. Distribute beanbags.
6. Call out a number to one child and have him throw the beanbag to the numbered square and hop or jump to it.
7. Distribute the balls, call out numbers to each child and challenge him to hop or jump to the numbered square and bounce the ball the number of time indicated by the number on the square.

TEACHER-TO-TEACHER TIP

- As the children's number recognition skills increase, write new numbers on paper and tape them over any permanent ones on the grid. Consider making a request from your director or principal to have a permanent hopscotch grid painted on your outdoor hardtop. On another day, teach interested children the traditional hopscotch game. With older children, consider having them bounce the ball to two separate squares and add the numbers.

Children's Books

Jump, Frog, Jump! by Robert Kalan (a Spanish version is also available)
Ten Black Dots by Donald Crews
Ten in a Bed by Mary Rees

ASSESSMENT

To assess the children's learning, consider the following:

- Did the child recognize the numbers on the grid?
- Can the child balance while hopping and jumping in the squares?

Margery Kranyik Fermino, West Roxbury, MA

Math Racers

5+

LEARNING OBJECTIVES

The children will:

1. Work on addition and subtraction while playing an outdoor racing game.
2. Reinforce theircounting skills.

Materials

two baskets or
  paper bags with
  handles
a dozen or more
  plastic eggs or
  small plastic
  balls
outdoor play yard
  or large indoor
  play room

VOCABULARY

addition   plus   race   subtraction
minus

PREPARATION

- Divide the children into two lines at one end of the play yard. Make two piles of balls or eggs at the other end of the play yard.

WHAT TO DO

1. Give the first two children in the lines the baskets or bags.
2. Begin the race by calling out an arithmetic problem, such as "2 plus 1!"
3. Children race to fill their bags or baskets with the correct number of eggs or balls to equal the answer. Have the children race back and count out their answers to see if they are correct.
4. Give each child one or more turns at the race.

TEACHER-TO-TEACHER TIPS

- To play the same game with younger children, call out a number instead of a math problem.
- Show children math problems on paper, and relate them to the racing game. Explain how "2 + 1 = 3" is the same as putting two eggs into the basket, plus putting another egg into the basket, which equals three eggs in the basket.

ASSESSMENT

To assess the children's learning, consider the following:

- Can the children recognize an addition equation?
- Are the children able to add small numbers?

Sarah Stasik, Bent Mountain, VA

Children's Books

365 Penguins by
Jean-Luc Fromental
and Joëlle Jolivet
Fun with Counting by
Jenny Ackland
Safari Park by
Stuart J. Murphy

Numbers on Parade

5+

LEARNING OBJECTIVES

The children will:

1. Learn to count to 11.
2. Learn to recognize the numbers 1–11.

Materials

22 pieces of 12" x
18" card stock
hole punch
markers or pencils
yarn
paint
paintbrushes
5" number cards
1–11

VOCABULARY

number names   sandwich board   set   sign
1–11

PREPARATION

- Punch two holes at the top of 22 card stock pieces.
- Draw large outlines of numbers 1–11 on 11 pieces of the card stock.
- Cut 22 12" lengths of yarn.

WHAT TO DO

1. Ask a group of children to paint in the numbers drawn on the card stock. Ask another group to paint a set of shapes on the other card stock pieces, so when the children finish, they have a picture of one item for the 1 number card, a picture of 2 items for the 2 number card, and so on.
2. When dry, help the children match the number cards with the painted sets.
3. Tie the matching cards together, leaving enough space for them to fit over a child's shoulders, like a sandwich-board sign. The number card should be facing so that it hangs over the child's front, and the set card should be hanging against the child's back, visible to the child behind him.
4. Ask the children to slip them on and get in order. March around outside singing the song. After each time the song is sung, stop marching and shout out, "One, two, three, four, five, six, seven, eight, nine, 10, 11!"

Numbers on Parade by Susan Oldham Hill

We are numbers on parade
We march in grand formation.
We love to count and count some
more

All around the station.
One, two, three, four, five, six, seven,
Eight, nine, ten, eleven.
We are numbers on parade,
All in grand formation!

Children's Books

Count! by
Denise Fleming
How Many Snails? by
Paul Giganti, Jr.
Parade by
Donald Crews

ASSESSMENT

To assess the children's learning, consider the following:

- Can the children name the numbers on the set of number cards?
- Give the children number cards for 1–5. Can they put them order?

Susan Oldham Hill, Lakeland, FL

Buried Numbers

3+

LEARNING OBJECTIVES

The children will:
1. Learn numbers by their shape.
2. Use sensory clues to identify shapes.
3. Improve their small motor skills.

Materials

plastic or wood
    numbers
sandbox
blindfolds
    (optional)

VOCABULARY

bury	dig	sand
coin	number names	treasure

PREPARATION

● Bury different numbers in the sandbox.

WHAT TO DO

1. Work with one child, or a few children, at a time. Ask each child to close her eyes (or use a blindfold is the child is willing). Tell the child that she is going to be digging for treasure.
2. Tell each child to dig in the sand until she finds a number, then feel it all over and tell you what number it is.
   Note: To add a bit of fun, bury several play coins in the sand for the children to dig up and count.

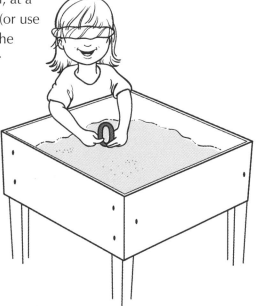

POEM

Sand Pies by Anne Adeney
Hot sand pies to sell,
Hot sand pies to sell,
Pat them down tightly,
And turn them out well.

Children's Books

I Spy Treasure Hunt by
    Jean Marzollo
*Not So Buried Treasure:
The Berenstain Bears* by
Stan and Jan Berenstain
Sand by Ellen Prager

ASSESSMENT

To assess the children's learning, consider the following:
● Can the children identify numbers by touch?
● Can the children identify differences in numbers by touch?

Anne Adeney, Plymouth, England, United Kingdom

Buried Treasure

4+

LEARNING OBJECTIVES

The children will:

1. Use their five senses.
2. Develop their critical thinking skills.
3. Identify and match like numbers.

Materials

plastic numbers,
1–5 (10" or
larger works
well)
sand table or tub
of sand
10 number cards
10 sand toys such
as shovel, pail,
sifter, scoop, and
so on

VOCABULARY

dig   find   sand
feel   numbers   touch

PREPARATION

- Tape a number card on each sand toy.
- Display the sand toys near the sand table so the numbers are showing.
- Bury the five plastic numbers beneath the sand.

WHAT TO DO

1. Ask the children to identify the numbers on the sand toys.
2. Explain to the children that there are matching numbers buried in the sand table. Challenge the children to dig through the sand to find the plastic numbers.
3. Encourage the children to feel the numbers they find and try to identify them before they lift them from the sand.
4. Have the children display each number they find beside the sand toy with the matching number. Congratulate the children as they locate numbers and match them.
5. Remind the children to hide the numbers in the sand so the table is ready for other children to use.

TEACHER-TO-TEACHER TIP

- For older children, use numbers 1–10 or print a number word on the sand toy and have the children match numbers with number words.

ASSESSMENT

To assess the children's learning, consider the following:

- Can the child identify numbers by touch only?
- Can the child match the number she pulled from the sand to the matching number attached to one of the sand toys?

Children's Books

*Blast Off! A Space
Counting Book* by
Norma Cole
Monster Math by
Grace Maccarone
Ten in a Bed by
Penny Dale

Mary J. Murray, Mazomanie, WI

Sink and Float

LEARNING OBJECTIVES

The children will:
1. Explore the concept of sinking and floating.
2. Recognize numbers.
3. Develop their oral language skills.

Materials

plastic numbers 1–9 that will float

numbers 1–10 that will sink (numbers 1–10 painted on smooth stones or printed on ceramic tiles with permanent marker)

VOCABULARY

float	sink	swim	water
numbers			

PREPARATION

- Print or paint the numbers on the heavy materials listed to the left and let dry.
- Place all the materials at the water table.

WHAT TO DO

1. Invite the children to explore with the numbers at the water table.
2. As the children explore, have them identify which numbers float and which numbers sink.
3. Encourage the children to talk about the various numbers using sentences to describe each number. "Plastic number 2 floats on top of the water. The number 4 stone sinks to the bottom."
4. When the children are finished playing, have them display all the numbers on a table nearby so the next group of children may see if they sink or float.

TEACHER-TO-TEACHER TIP

- Invite older children to sink and float pairs of numbers together to form a new number, and then say the new number aloud: "A two with a four is 24."

ASSESSMENT

To assess the children's learning, consider the following:
- Do the children understand the concepts of sinking and floating?
- Display all the numbers in the water. Gather a group of children around as you point out various numbers. Can each child identify the numbers?

Mary J. Murray, Mazomanie, WI

Children's Books

Animal Babies 1, 2, 3 by Eve Spencer
My Little Counting Book by Roger Priddy
Pigs from 1–10 by Arthur Geisert

Water Numbers

4+

LEARNING OBJECTIVES

The children will:

1. Use water to reinforce their knowledge of numbers.
2. Improve their small motor control.
3. Improve concentration.
4. Learn to follow instructions.

Materials

water
small spray bottle
for each child

VOCABULARY

squirt   number names

PREPARATION

● Make large chalk numbers in an empty playground or paved yard.
● Fill water guns or spray bottles with water.

WHAT TO DO

1. Show the children how to draw numbers by squirting water carefully around the chalk numbers, making sure that they start the number in the correct place.
2. When the children have better control of the water, challenge them to draw water numbers without the chalk outline to follow.

TEACHER-TO-TEACHER TIP

● Some children simply do not have the motor skills to do this at four or even five years old. If this is making them discouraged, ask these children to draw you a water picture instead. This does not require nearly as much accuracy.

ASSESSMENT

To assess the children's learning, consider the following:

● Does each child follow your instructions on making water numbers?
● Can the children concentrate long enough to complete several numbers?
● Do the children remember where to start when drawing each number?

Anne Adeney, Plymouth, England, United Kingdom

Children's Books

I Spy Little Numbers by Jean Marzollo
Mother Goose Numbers on the Loose by Leo and Diane Dillon
Ten Black Dots by Donald Crews

Toy Phone Typing

LEARNING OBJECTIVES

The children will:
1. Recognize numbers.
2. Write numbers.
3. Verbalize the names of the numbers.

Materials

toy phones
discarded cell
    phones or
    landline phones
    (with keypads)
chalkboard and
    chalk or dry-
    erase boards and
    markers (paper
    and pencil will
    also work)

VOCABULARY

dial   order   phone call   sequence

PREPARATION

- Group the children in pairs and set out one phone and writing board per pair.

WHAT TO DO

1. Tell the children that they will be making "phone calls," but to do this they need to know the "phone numbers."
2. Have one child in the pair write a sequence of numbers in a straight line on the writing board.
3. The second child then types the numbers into the phone in order as written, saying each number aloud as he types.
4. Once he has entered all the numbers, the child can pretend to call someone.
5. Invite the children to take turns writing and dialing.

TEACHER-TO-TEACHER TIP

- Be sure to have enough phones; otherwise, use this as a center activity. Three in a group does not work as well as two.

ASSESSMENT

To assess the children's learning, consider the following:
- Can the children write some numbers?
- Can the children dial the numbers in the order they are written?
- Can the children speak the numbers aloud as they dial?

Jaclyn Miller, Mishawaka, IN

Children's Books

Curious George Learns to Count from 1 to 100 by H.A. Rey
I Spy Little Numbers by Jean Marzollo
My Fist Numbers: Let's Get Counting by DK Publishing

Washing Line

4+

LEARNING OBJECTIVES

The children will:

1. Practice sequencing numbers.
2. Improve their small motor skills.
3. Build life skills.

clothesline
spring-style
   clothespins
marker
assortment of small
   children's
   clothes
picture of clothes
   hanging on a
   clothesline

VOCABULARY

clothespin   order   washing line

PREPARATION

- Put up a clothesline at an appropriate level.
- Mark clothespins with numbers 1–10.

WHAT TO DO

1. Engage the children in a discussion about different ways of doing laundry. Show the children pictures of clothes hanging on a clothesline.
2. Set out the clothespins. Show the children how to open the clothespins and use them to hang things on the line.
3. Get the children to lay out the clothespins in numerical order, letting younger children match a printed number sequence.
4. Mix up the clothespins again and ask the children to pin the clothes on the line in numeric order.
5. Hang the paintings to dry, instead of clothes.
6. In warm weather, children will enjoy washing the clothes first and hanging them outdoors to dry.

TEACHER-TO-TEACHER TIP

- Use real baby clothing rather than doll's clothes, reassuring the children that everybody wears clothes and needs to wash them.

ASSESSMENT

To assess the children's learning, consider the following:

- Can the children manipulate the clothespins to hang up the clothing?
- Can the children sequence the clothespins in numerical order?
- Do the children understand why clothes need to be hung up?

Anne Adeney, Plymouth, England, United Kingdom

Children's Books

The Day Jimmy's Boa Ate the Wash by Trinka Hakes Noble
Little Grey Rabbit's Washing Day by Alison Uttley
Mrs. McNosh Hangs Up Her Wash by Sarah Weeks
Sudsy Mom's Washing Spree by Wakiko Sato

Yarn Numbers

4+

LEARNING OBJECTIVES

The children will:

1. Develop number recognition.
2. Learn how to form numbers.

Materials

large number
  stencils
marker
paper
yarn
school glue

VOCABULARY

curve   line   numbers   straight

PREPARATION

- Trace around the large numbers or number stencils. Make one number for each child.
- Cut pieces of yarn.

WHAT TO DO

1. Give each child pieces of yarn, glue, and a sheet of paper with one large block number on it.
2. Ask the children to glue the yarn pieces on top of the numbers, taking care to follow the shapes of the numbers.

ASSESSMENT

To assess the children's learning, consider the following:

- Use pieces of yarn to make a number on the floor. Can the children call out the number you made? Continue doing this until you review all of the numbers that you are currently studying.
- Can the children create numbers on the floor using items from the classroom?

Erin Huffstetler, Maryville, TN

Children's Books

Chicka Chicka Boom Boom by Bill Martin, Jr.
Five Little Monkeys Jumping on the Bed by Eileen Christelow
How Do Dinosaurs Count to Ten? by Jane Yolen
Ten Little Dinosaurs by Pattie L. Schnetzler

Post That Number

LEARNING OBJECTIVES

The children will:

1. Practice counting 1–10.
2. Match numbers and amounts from 1–10.
3. Practice their small motor skills.

Materials

small envelopes
thick marker
flat objects (like
   sock sorters or
   plastic coins) to
   place inside
   envelopes
empty shoebox
sharp knife or
   scissors (adult
   only)
resealable plastic
   bags
poster paint
   (optional)

VOCABULARY

checker   envelope   mailbox   postage

PREPARATION

- Cut a 1" x 5" slit at one end of the shoebox. This will be the mailbox where the children "mail" their letters. It can be painted like a mailbox or left plain. Or, use a play mailbox (at toy and thrift stores).
- Write a number from 1–10 on each envelope.
- Place the flat objects to be counted in the resealable bag.

WHAT TO DO

1. Tape the bottom of the shoebox securely to a table so that the slit is at the top. Show the children how to do the activity.
2. Select an envelope and let the children tell you what number is on it. Open the resealable bag and pull out a handful of flat objects.
3. Place the objects inside the envelope one at a time. Count the objects aloud as you put them in the envelope. Do not lick or seal the envelope.
4. Ask a child to "mail" the envelope in the shoebox.
5. Before each child drops an envelope in the mailbox, open it and count out the objects again to check for the proper "postage." Say things like, "Uh-oh! Not enough postage! Ah! The right amount of postage. Oops, too much postage in this one!"
6. Select different children to be the postage checker. They enjoy being in charge and appreciate being acknowledged.

ASSESSMENT

To assess the children's learning, consider the following:

- Are the children focusing on the task?
- Are the children able to count out correct amounts?

Children's Books

How Do Dinosaurs Count to Ten? by Jane Yolen
Ten, Nine, Eight by Molly Bang

Kay Flowers, Summerfield, OH

Edible Numbers

4+

LEARNING OBJECTIVES

The children will:
1. Learn basic numbers in a fun, creative way.
2. Learn to follow simple directions.

Materials

sheet of waxed paper per child

one round of ready-made biscuit dough per child (Use cans with 8 biscuits because they are easier to mold than the large, specialized biscuits.)

smocks or old T-shirts to cover clothes

oven or toaster oven

baking sheet (or one pie plate per child)

raisins or chocolate chips (optional)

VOCABULARY

edible   number names

PREPARATION

- It is helpful to have the biscuit dough wrapped in the waxed paper to pass out.

WHAT TO DO

1. Have the children wash their hands.
2. On waxed paper, let the children roll and form the biscuit dough into long snakes with their hands.
3. Help the children form a number. Although most numbers can be formed without breaking the dough, some will need to be shaped by breaking the dough in pieces.
4. Extend the experience by having the children add raisins or chocolate chips to the dough (one raisin for the number 1, two for 2, and so on).
5. Bake according to package directions. Enjoy the math snack!
   Safety Note: Before serving any food, especially peanut butter, check for allergies.

SONG

Bake a One by Donna Alice Patton
(Tune: "Here We Go 'Round the Mulberry Bush")
This is the way we bake a one,
Bake a one, bake a one.
This is the way we bake a one
So early in the morning.

(Change the number for later verses.)

Children's Books

The Cat in Numberland by Ivar Ekeland
My Little Counting Book by Roger Priddy
My Very First Book of Numbers by Eric Carle

ASSESSMENT

To assess the children's learning, consider the following:
- Are the children able to shape the biscuit dough into numbers?
- Did the children get a "feel" for how a number is formed?
- Did the children remember the dough shapes when they began to write numbers?

Donna Alice Patton, Hillsboro, OH

How Many Spoonfuls?

4+

LEARNING OBJECTIVES

The children will:
1. Practice one-to-one correspondence with objects.
2. Learn the concept of one more.

Materials

foods eaten with a
  spoon: cereal
  and milk,
  pudding,
  applesauce,
  yogurt, gelatin,
  ice cream
spoons
bowls
paper
pencils
blocks

VOCABULARY

| applesauce | cereal | milk | spoon |
| bite | chew | pudding | |

WHAT TO DO

1. Give the children cereals, puddings, applesauce, or other foods that require a spoon to eat.
   Note: Before serving any food, especially peanut butter, check for allergies.
2. Tell the children they will be counting how many spoonfuls it will take to eat their snack.
3. Have small blocks at the table and near the children. Each time they take a spoonful of snack, they take one block from the pile.
4. When they are all done eating, they can count how many blocks they have and this will tell them how many bites they've eaten.
5. More advanced children can try to predict how many spoonfuls it will take to eat their food.

SONG

The Breakfast Song by Monica Hay Cook
(Tune: "Here We Go 'Round the Mulberry Bush")
This is the way we use a spoon, use a spoon, use a spoon.
This is the way we use a spoon, so early in the morning.
This is the way we take a bite, take a bite, take a bite.
This is the way we take a bite, so early in the morning.

(additional verses)
This is the way we chew our food…
This is the way we swallow our food…
This is the way we count the bites…

Children's Books

Food for Thought by
  Saxton Freyman
Fun with Counting by
  Jenny Ackland
*What Do You Want in
  Your Cereal Bowl?* by
  William Boniface

ASSESSMENT

To assess the children's learning, consider the following:
- When given objects, can the children use them to create another set (one-to-one correspondence)?
- Given a number of objects, can the child count to 10?

Monica Hay Cook, Tucson, AZ

Nibbled Pretzel Numbers

4+

LEARNING OBJECTIVES

The children will:

1. Recognize number shapes.
2. Produce number shapes.

Materials

regular size twisted pretzels (not mini-pretzels)
napkins

VOCABULARY

crumbs	napkin	salt
display	nibble	shape

WHAT TO DO

1. Give the children paper napkins and about three pretzels each, and take some for yourself. Nibble tiny bites out of a pretzel so that the remainder is in the shape of a number.
   Note: Before serving any food, especially peanut butter, check for allergies.
2. Place the nibbled pretzel on your napkin so the outline of the number is clearly seen.
3. Let the children tell you what number they recognize. Nibble another pretzel into a different number so the children see there are other possibilities.
4. Enjoy the laughter with the children as they nibble their pretzels into numbers and display their creations on their napkins.
5. You can make this activity a bit more challenging by using straight pretzel sticks. The sticks will need to be broken or bitten into shorter lengths in order to make rounded edges. Napkins help keep the snack area neat.

SONG

The Pretzel Song by Kay Flowers
(Tune: "Bumpin' Up and Down in My Little Red Wagon")
One salty, two salty, three salty pretzels.
Four salty, five salty, six salty pretzels.
Seven salty, eight salty, nine salty pretzels.
Ten salty pretzels I see.

Children's Books

Count and See by Tana Hoban
Size by Henry Arthur Pluckrose
Spot's Colors, Shapes, and Numbers by Eric Hill

ASSESSMENT

To assess the children's learning, consider the following:

- Can the children recognize number shapes made by others?
- Can the children create their own number shapes?

Kay Flowers, Summerfield, OH

Raisin Numbers

4+

LEARNING OBJECTIVES
The children will:
1. Reinforce number recognition.
2. Practice their small motor skills.

Materials

raisins
small paper cups
plain crackers
peanut butter
plastic knives
toothpicks
number cards, if
   required

VOCABULARY
cracker   raisins   spread

PREPARATION
- Put raisins into small paper cups.

WHAT TO DO
1. Give each child a cracker.
2. Ask the children to spread peanut butter onto their cracker.
   Safety Note: Before serving any food, especially peanut butter, check for allergies.
3. Draw numbers in the peanut butter with a toothpick for younger children. Ask the children to put raisins along the line to make the number.
4. Older children can make raisin numbers by copying from number cards or making them from memory.
5. Ask the children to identify the numbers when they are served at snack time.

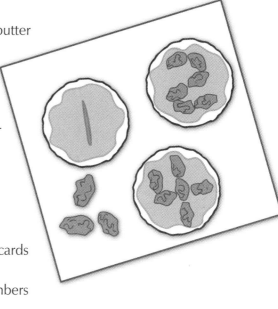

TEACHER-TO-TEACHER TIP
- Ask the children to line up the crackers in numerical order before they eat their snack.

ASSESSMENT
To assess the children's learning, consider the following:
- Can each child identify the numbers made with raisins?
- Can the children follow the lines and make recognizable numbers?

Anne Adeney, Plymouth, England, United Kingdom

Children's Books

Count! by
Denise Fleming
Food for Thought by
Saxton Freyman
*Honey's Peanut Butter
Adventure* by
Tom C. Greer and
Laurie A. Faust

Poems

"Hot Cross Buns"
"Five Currant Buns in a
Baker's Shop"

Snack Cakes

4+

LEARNING OBJECTIVES

The children will:
1. Practice number formation.
2. Enhance social skills.
3. Use their five senses.

Materials

rice cakes
spreadable topping
  such as peanut
  butter, softened
  cream cheese,
  or frosting
small edibles such
  as raisins, seeds,
  nuts, small fruit
  pieces
plastic butter
  knives
number chart
  showing
  numbers 1–10

VOCABULARY

| eat | munch | raisins | seed |
| fruit | peanut butter | rice cake | spread |

WHAT TO DO

1. Invite the children to spread a topping on their rice cakes.
2. Ask the children to select their favorite number from the number chart.
3. Encourage the children to use the small edible pieces of fruit and nuts to form the number on their rice cakes.
   Safety Note: Before serving any food, especially nuts, check for allergies.
4. Invite each child to show and tell about her snack, and then allow the children to munch away on this fun snack.

TEACHER-TO-TEACHER TIP

● Use graham crackers in place of rice cakes for a less expensive treat.

ASSESSMENT

To assess the children's learning, consider the following:
● Can each child identify the numbers on the number chart?
● Provide each child with a plateful of small edibles. Can she form numbers by arranging the edible snacks on her plate?

Mary J. Murray, Mazomanie, WI

Children's Books

All About 1 2 3 by
  Ruth Thomson
Number Munch! by
  Charles Reasoner
What's for Lunch? by
  Eric Carle

What's Cooking?

4+

LEARNING OBJECTIVES

The children will:

1. Follow directions to make a recipe.
2. Count a specified number of ingredients.

Materials

poster board
marker
paper plates
salad ingredients
pizza ingredients

VOCABULARY

directions   half   ingredients   recipe

WHAT TO DO

1. Explain that numbers are used all the time: to tell time, to buy food, to make food. Tell the children that they will make a salad and a pizza by identifying numbers, counting the proper amount of ingredients, and following directions. **Safety Note:** Before serving any food, especially peanut butter, check for allergies.
2. Show the children the recipes and the ingredients on the tables. Read through each recipe as a class. Invite the children to follow the recipes below:

Salad
1 paper plate
2 leaves of lettuce
3 chunks of cheese
4 cherry tomatoes
5 olives
6 sliced carrots
7 croutons

Directions
Tear the lettuce into pieces on the plate.
Place 3 pieces of cheese, 4 tomatoes, 5 olives, 6 carrots, and 7 croutons on top.

Pizza
1 English muffin (already sliced in half)
2 scoops of tomato sauce
4 green peppers
6 pieces of cheese
8 pieces of pepperoni
10 olives

Directions
Open up the muffin.
Spread 1 scoop of tomato sauce on each muffin.
Place 2 green peppers on each muffin.
Place 3 pieces of cheese on each muffin.
Place 4 pieces of pepperoni on each muffin.
Place 5 olives on each muffin.
Bake on a cookie sheet for 10 minutes in a 400 F oven (adult-only step).

ASSESSMENT

To assess the children's learning, consider the following:

- Can the children count the ingredients in their salads and pizzas?
- Can the children follow the directions to make salads and pizzas?

Angela Hawkins, Denver, CO

Children's Books

Eating the Alphabet by Lois Ehlert
Food for Thought by Saxton Freyman
My Very First Book of Numbers by Eric Carle

Eating Numbers

5+

LEARNING OBJECTIVES

The children will:
1. Learn numbers 1–5.
2. Differentiate between smallest and largest.
3. Develop their motor skills.

Materials

blackboard and chalk, dry-erase board and dry-erase marker, or chart paper and marker
iced mini-muffins (five per child)
small paper cups
raisins

VOCABULARY

even	number names	odd	smallest
largest	1–5		

WHAT TO DO

1. Write the numbers 1–5 on a blackboard, dry-erase board, or chart paper. Point to each one as you say the number aloud.
2. Explain that the number one is the smallest number and number five is the largest number.
3. Give each child five mini-muffins. Give them a cup with 15 raisins. Ask the children to number the muffins from 1–5 by placing one raisin on the first muffin, two raisins on the next muffin, and so on.
4. Have the children arrange the muffins from smallest to largest based on the number of raisins, and then eat their math experience for snack!
   Safety Note: Before serving any food, especially peanut butter, check for allergies.

ASSESSMENT

To assess the children's learning, consider the following:
● Can the children count from 1–5 (or 1–10)?
● When you say a number, can the child hold up that many muffins?

Randi Lynn Mrvos, Lexington, KY

Children's Books

The Crayon Counting Book by Pam Munoz Ryan and Jerry Pallotta
I Spy Little Numbers by Jean Marzollo
One Red Sun: A Counting Book by Ezra Jack Keats

Sweet Numbers

5+

LEARNING OBJECTIVES
The children will:
1. Identify numbers 1–5.
2. Count numbers 1–5.
3. Put numbers in sequence.

Materials

small paper cups
(five per child)
jellybeans (five
different colors;
15 jellybeans
per child)
snack-size plastic
baggies (one per
child)
number flash cards
manipulatives,
such as counters

VOCABULARY
group   order   sort

PREPARATION
- Place 15 jelly beans in a baggie for each child. Make sure you have one of one color, two of another color, and so on until you finish with five of another color.

WHAT TO DO
1. Show the children flash cards with numbers 1–5, and identify each one. Use manipulatives to coordinate with each number to show how many of something each number represents.
2. Show each number (one at a time), and ask the children to identify them.
3. Distribute five cups, and one baggie with 15 jellybeans to each child.
4. Tell the children to sort the jellybeans according to their color, and put each colored group in one of the cups, for example, all the pink jellybeans in one cup.
5. After the children finish sorting the jelly beans, have them count each group in each cup. Help them write that number on the cup with a marker. Continue until they have counted all of the jelly beans and numbered all of their cups.
6. Ask the children to order the cups from 1–5. As a reward for their hard work, the children can eat the jelly beans.
   Safety Note: Before serving any food, check for allergies.

ASSESSMENT
To assess the children's learning, consider the following:
- Can the children identify numbers 1–5?
- Can the children count numbers 1–5 by counting jellybeans according to their color?
- Did the children learn the sequence of numbers by putting the numbered cups in the correct order?

Children's Books

*1-2-3: A Child's First
Counting Book* by
Alison Jay
Count! by
Denise Fleming
Counting Colors by
Roger Priddy

Randi Lynn Mrvos, Lexington, KY

The Birthday Graph

4+

LEARNING OBJECTIVES

The children will:

1. Learn to read a graph.
2. Learn the months of the year.

Materials

paper
scissors (adult only)
markers
large chart paper
 divided into 12
 sections
list of the children's
 birth months
glue sticks

VOCABULARY

graph   month names   number names
                                     1–12

PREPARATION

● Make name cards for the children about 8" long.
● Label the 12 sections of the chart paper with the months of the year.

WHAT TO DO

1. Ask the children to tell which month they were born in. Help any who are unsure.
2. Show each child how to glue his name card under the correct month to show his birth month.
3. Continue until all the children have glued their names on the graph.
4. When the graph is dry, hang it up in the classroom and compare the results.

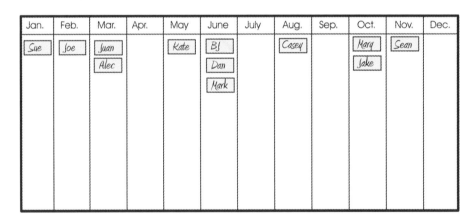

Jan.	Feb.	Mar.	Apr.	May	June	July	Aug.	Sep.	Oct.	Nov.	Dec.
Sue	Joe	Juan		Kate	BJ		Casey		Mary	Sean	
		Alec			Dan				Jake		
					Mark						

TEACHER-TO-TEACHER TIP

● To extend this activity, bring some simple graphs from newspapers to discuss. For snack, serve birthday cupcakes with candles to blow out.

ASSESSMENT

To assess the children's learning, consider the following:

● Can the children discuss the results of the graph?
● Can the children tell you which month has the most names? The fewest names? Are any months with no names? Do any months have the same number of names?

Children's Books

Carl's Birthday by
 Alexandra Day
Happy Birthday, Moon
 by Frank Asch
Spot's Birthday Party by
 Eric Hill

Song

Sing "Happy Birthday"
with the children.

Susan Oldham Hill, Lakeland, FL

Five Little Kites

3+

Materials

paper
scissors (adult only)
markers

LEARNING OBJECTIVES

The children will:
1. Learn to count to five.
2. Learn numbers through fingerplay.

VOCABULARY

fly   kite   number names
                                                                1–5

PREPARATION

- Make five 9" x 12" kite shapes in different colors, numbering them 1–5.
- Make five 3" x 4" kite shapes, numbering them 1–5.

WHAT TO DO

1. Teach the children the following fingerplay:

   Five Little Kites by Susan Oldham Hill
   One little kite up in the air,
   Two little kites make a pair.
   Three little kites floating in the sky,
   Four little kites zoom way up high.
   Five little kites bobbing up and down,
   Swirling, twirling, to the ground.

2. Choose five children to sit in front of the group holding the kite shapes in order from one to five.
3. Ask the child holding the kite marked one to stand and lift the kite shape up as the children say the first line of the fingerplay.
4. Ask each child in turn to stand and move his kite shape for each line of the fingerplay.
5. Ask the children watching to say the fingerplay and hold up the correct number of fingers for each line.

ASSESSMENT

To assess the children's learning, consider the following:
- Can each child name the numbers on the small kite number cards?
- Can the children hold up the correct number of fingers during the fingerplay?

Susan Oldham Hill, Lakeland, FL

Children's Books

Curious George Flies a Kite by H. A. Rey
The Kite by Mary Packard
Kite Flying by Grace Lin

Number Chant

4+

LEARNING OBJECTIVES

The children will:

1. Count from 1–10 using their fingers on both hands.
2. Recognize that there are five fingers on each hand.

Materials

no materials necessary

VOCABULARY

finger   hand   numbers names
                                                   1–5

PREPARATION

● Learn the song below. Practice demonstrating the numbers with your fingers.

WHAT TO DO

1. Review counting from 1–10 with hands in the air, showing the correct number of fingers for each number.
2. Sing the following song, showing the correct number of fingers at the appropriate times. Have the children mirror your hand motions with the song.

1, 2, 3, 4, 5 by Christina Chilcote
(Tune: "Head, Shoulders, Knees, and Toes")

1, 2, 3, 4, and 5, 4 and 5, (show
    appropriate fingers)
1, 2, 3, 4, and 5, 4 and 5,
All the fingers on my one hand (hold
    up one hand)
Add up to 1, 2, 3, 4, 5, 4 and 5.
6, 7, 8, and 9, 8 and 9, (show
    appropriate fingers)

6, 7, 8, and 9, 8 and 9,
Add one more finger
And you will have 10. (hold up both
    hands.)
Clap your hands and (clap hands.)
Sing again!

3. Once the children are confident with the numbers and fingers, explain that the group will sing the song three times in a row, starting slowly the first time and increasing the speed and rhythm of the song the second and third time.
4. Sing the song three times, increasing the speed of the song each time. By the end of the third time, everyone should be laughing and giggling at the silliness of the effort.

Children's Books

Duckie's Ducklings by
    Frances Barry
My Little Counting Book
    by Roger Priddy
One Naked Baby by
    Maggie Smith

ASSESSMENT

To assess the children's learning, consider the following:

● Can the children slowly count from 1–10, demonstrating the numbers with their fingers?
● If you ask to see five fingers, do the children hold up one hand?

Christina Chilcote, New Freedom, PA

10 Little Children, Jumping 5+

LEARNING OBJECTIVES
The children will:
1. Learn to follow simple directions.
2. Reinforce counting number 1–10.

Materials

no materials necessary

VOCABULARY

clap	jump	skip	wave
dance	laugh	smile	walk
frown			

WHAT TO DO

1. Have the children stand in a circle. Show them how to count from 1–10 on their fingers.
2. Begin singing the first verse of the song while holding up the appropriate number of fingers. Encourage the children to hold up the correct number of fingers and sing along.

Little Children Jumping by Sarah Stasik
(Tune: "Bumping Up and Down in My Little Red Wagon")
One little, two little, three little children,
Four little, five little, six little children,
Seven little, eight little, nine little children,
Ten little children jumping!

3. Have the children jump. Then say "Now, let's do clapping." Sing the second verse of the song.

One little, two little, three little children,
Four little, five little, six little children,
Seven little, eight little, nine little children,
Ten little children clapping!

4. Repeat the song with other actions: hopping, skipping, waving, smiling, frowning, walking, laughing, and dancing.

TEACHER-TO-TEACHER TIP
- Let the children take turns calling out the next action to perform.

ASSESSMENT
To assess the children's learning, consider the following:
- Can the children count from 1–10 using their fingers?
- Can the children sing the song from memory?

Sarah Stasik, Bent Mountain, VA

Children's Books

1-2-3: A Child's First Counting Book by Alison Jay
1, 2, 3 to the Zoo by Eric Carle
All About 1 2 3 by Ruth Thomson

Five Brand New Pets

5+

LEARNING OBJECTIVES

The children will:

1. Learn subtraction from five.
2. Learn about pet stores.
3. Learn about financial transactions.

Materials

five or more soft toy pets, including a cat and dog
five or more dollar bills, real or imitation

VOCABULARY

dollar   kitten   pet store   puppy

WHAT TO DO

1. Engage the children in a conversation about pet stores; about how they work and what they sell.
2. Teach the children the following poem:

Five Brand New Pets by Anne Adeney
Five brand new pets in an old pet store,
A kitten, a puppy, and many more.
Along came (child's name) with a
* dollar one day,*
Bought a brand new pet and took
* it right away.*
Four brand new pets in an old pet
* store,*

A kitten, a puppy, and many more.
Along came (another child's name)
* with a dollar one day,*
Bought a brand new pet and took
* it right away.*

Three brand new pets in an old
* pet store....*

3. Place five soft toy pets in the middle of the group and use them to act out the rhyme.
4. Younger children can count how many pets are left each time.
5. At the end, ask the children how many dollars the pet store owner has made.
6. Help the children count the money the pet store owner received.

TEACHER-TO-TEACHER TIP

● Sing the song with the same number of pets as you have children, so every child has a turn buying each time. Extend the activity by labeling the pets with different prices, from $1 to $5, then adding up the costs.

Children's Books

Best Pet Yet by Louise Tidd
Oh, the Pets You Can Get by Tish Rabe
Pet Store Subtraction by Simone T. Ribke

ASSESSMENT

To assess the children's learning, consider the following:

● Can the children tell you why they need the dollar in this song?
● Can the children tell you where they would go and what they would need to do if they were to get a new pet?

> Anne Adeney, Plymouth, England, United Kingdom

Index of Children's Books

Index

ISBN 978-0-87659-092-8
Gryphon House | 16247 | PB

ISBN 978-0-87659-088-1
Gryphon House | 13467 | PB

ISBN 978-0-87659-237-3
Gryphon House | 13963 | PB

ISBN 978-0-87659-238-0
Gryphon House | 14964 | PB

ISBN 978-0-87659-285-4
Gryphon House | 18595 | PB

ISBN 978-0-87659-013-3
Gryphon House | 13614 | PB

the **GIANT** encyclopedia of theme activities for children 2 to 5

Over 600 Favorite Activities Created by Teachers for Teachers

ISBN 978-0-87659-166-6
Gryphon House | 19216 | PB

The **GIANT** Encyclopedia of Math Activities For Children 3 to 6

Written by Teachers for Teachers

Edited by Kathy Charner, Maureen Murphy, and Charlie Clark

ISBN 978-0-87659-044-7
Gryphon House | 16948 | PB

The **GIANT** Encyclopedia of Circle Time and Group Activities for Children 3 to 6

Over 600 Favorite Circle Time Activities Created by Teachers for Teachers

Edited by Kathy Charner

ISBN 978-0-87659-181-9
Gryphon House | 16413 | PB

The **GIANT** Encyclopedia of Science Activities for Children 3 to 6

More Than 600 Science Activities Written by Teachers for Teachers

Edited by Kathy Charner

ISBN 978-0-87659-193-2
Gryphon House | 18325 | PB

The **GIANT** Encyclopedia of Art & Craft Activities for Children 3 to 6

More Than 500 Art & Craft Activities Written by Teachers for Teachers

Edited by Kathy Charner

ISBN 978-0-87659-209-0
Gryphon House | 16854 | PB

The GIANT Encyclopedia of Lesson Plans For Children 3 to 6
More Than 250 Lesson Plans Created by Teachers for Teachers
Edited by Kathy Charner, Maureen Murphy, and Charlie Clark

ISBN 978-0-87659-068-3
Gryphon House | 18345 | PB

The GIANT Encyclopedia of Monthly Activities For Children 3 to 6
Written by Teachers for Teachers
Edited by Kathy Charner, Maureen Murphy, and Charlie Clark

ISBN 978-0-87659-012-6
Gryphon House | 15002 | PB

The GIANT Encyclopedia of Transition Activities for Children 3 to 6
Over 600 Activities Created by Teachers for Teachers
Edited by Kathy Charner, Maureen Murphy, and Jennifer Ford

ISBN 978-0-87659-003-4
Gryphon House | 12635 | PB

The GIANT Encyclopedia of Learning Center Activities for Children 3 to 6
Over 600 Activities Created by Teachers for Teachers
Edited by Kathy Charner, Maureen Murphy, and Jennifer Ford

ISBN 978-0-87659-001-0
Gryphon House | 11325 | PB